OUT OF THIS WORLD

OUT OF THIS WORLD

The Illustrated Library of the Bizarre and Extraordinary

Editor: Perrott Phillips
Editorial assistants: Mundy Ellis/Robin Wilcox
Contributors: Colin Wilson/Angus Hall/Perrott Phillips/Roy Nash/
         Harry Weaver/Leslie Watkins/Ian Brown/Jeremy
         Pascall/Sally Brompton/Ian Ridpath
Design: Sarah Reynolds
Production Control: Phil Howard-Jones
Picture Research: Joanna Brindley/Paul Snelgrove
Editorial Director: Graham Donaldson
Cover Design: Harry W. Fass
Production Manager: Warren E. Bright

Contents

Out of This World

An American "tourist" on Mars	9
Just a matter of time	37
By H-bomb to the stars	65
Our new home among the stars	93

Bizarre

Exorcism—prelude to murder	13
The terror that howls	41
Voices from the dead	69
Chamber of horrors	97

Mystery

They strolled through a hole in time	17
The coffins have moved again!	47
I survived the royal massacre	75
Is this a photo of Christ?	103

Front Page

Kiss of death	23
The curse of the Kennedys	51
"It can't be true . . . they've shot Bobby!"	79
"I could not bear another loss"	107

Mythmakers

Grab your top hat . . . we're off to outer space!	29
Aaargh, the monster's got me!	57
Don't be beastly to the humans	85
When a monster says 'I love you. . .'	113

People

My life of booze, broads and bedlam	31
Empress who only wanted a baby	59
Romance that rocked an Empire	87
Give up this woman or leave the throne	115

"I wants to make your flesh creep."
The Fat Boy, *Pickwick Papers,* Chapter 8
—Charles Dickens

Introduction

Blessed by wealth and touched by genius, the Kennedys are America's 'Golden Family.' At one time, nothing seemed beyond their grasp—for power, prestige and an almost legendary glamor were all theirs. Yet a malign influence dogs their every step, striking tragically and unerringly at the peak of their triumphs. In this issue of OUT OF THIS WORLD, we follow the Curse of the Kennedys from its first, baleful appearance to the present moment and ask: Is it the price they have to pay for being the 'royal family' of the New World?

It was not an assassin's bullet which dealt a grievous blow to the English monarchy, but Cupid's arrow. When King Edward VIII fell in love with the American society beauty Wallis Simpson—and made it clear he intended to marry her–the 'establishment' reeled back in horror. For Mrs. Simpson had divorced her first husband and had married again. Under the unbending moral code of the British constitution, such a woman was 'unfit to be Queen.' We follow the extraordinary events of the royal romance in our *People* section, leading up to the final drama when Crown confronted Country.

Bizarre is almost an understatement when used to describe the frightening history of the Werewolf: the men who change by night into ravening predators. For, as our investigation shows, such creatures have actually existed outside men's fevered imaginations.

What are the powerful forces preventing us colonizing the stars? In our *Out of This World* section, we continue to explore the worlds *beyond* ours.

Even now, scientists are seriously discussing a revolutionary possibility: a colony suspended in space where earthly 'emigrants' will begin what could prove to be the perfect life away from it all. Read on. It is nearer than you think.

Lovers of the unexplained will be fascinated by the world-famous 'question marks' we have re-investigated under our *Mystery* heading. Consider . . . In France, two women walked through a 'hole in history' to find themselves back in the 18th century. In Germany, a woman saved from suicide turned out to be a 'living ghost'—a member of the Russian royal family supposedly all murdered by the Bolsheviks. In Italy, a photographer peered through a negative . . . to find he had miraculously 'photographed' Christ. And in Barbados, coffins started their own *danse macabre* when the dead refused to lie down. What is the truth about these mystifying incidents? You must be the judge.

So far, we have only touched on a fraction of the contents of Volume 3 of OUT OF THIS WORLD. In the *Mythmakers* department, for example, we take an affectionate look at the weird and wonderful ways in which artists have visualized space travel . . . and those Little Green Men from 'out there.'

To turn each page of this volume is to be amazed, to be stimulated, to be fascinated—truly an experience which is out of this world.

—Perrott Phillips

AN AMERICAN 'TOURIST' ON MARS

Like any keen holidaymaker, the Viking spacecraft started taking pictures as soon as it arrived. But these were 'snaps' of Mars. And they were just the start of an incredible 'working visit' by a machine with a brain, heart, skill . . . and a sense of humor.

The pictures were sharp and clearly defined. They showed a dull, rust-colored landscape strewn with rocks beneath a pink, cloudless sky. The color shots would never have won a photographic prize, even though they had cost more than $2 billion to 'snap'. Yet they were as historic and revolutionary as any pictures ever taken.

They came from 200 million miles away . . . from America's Viking 1 mission to Mars, one of the most spectacular and successful space probes ever achieved and a miracle of human talent and ingenuity.

The Viking was almost a 'thinking machine'. It survived a ten-month, 500-million-mile journey through interplanetary space before braking itself into orbit round Mars. Like a human being pondering what step to take next, it scanned the surface of the planet below to check the suitability of the proposed landing site. In the event, it turned out to be too rugged and Viking's own pictures helped the control team on earth to select a new one.

The orbiting vehicle released a lander which, with the help of a parachute and braking rockets, touched down intact on Mars—the first spacecraft ever to do so. Its three 'terminal descent engines'—each a cluster of 18 small nozzles, tilted outwards so as not to contaminate the soil samples to be taken later—ensured a soft landing. Sensors on the lander's 'foot pads' cut off the engines for touchdown. The date was July 20, 1976.

On the surface—almost like an eager, camera-toting tourist—the lander sent back the first close-up pictures of the Martian surface. Then, on command from earth, it began the more serious work: scientific experiments to throw new light on the origins of the solar

9

NASA

Centaur Parking Orbit

Stage 2 Separation

Bioshield Cap Jettison

Space Flight 305–360 days

Mars Orbit Insertion

Orbiter

Shroud Jettison

Entry 800,000 ft

Stage 1 Separation

Solid Rocket Motor Separation

Parachute Deployment 20,000 ft

Aeroshell Jettison

Terminal Descent 4000 ft

Launch Titan III/Centaur

Entry to Landing 5–10 minutes

NASA

High Gain S-Band Antenna (to Earth)

Seismometer

Facsimile Cameras (2)

Low-Gain S-Band Antenna

Meteorology

UHF Antenna

Roll Control Engines (4)

RTGs & Wind Covers (2 each)

Fuel Tanks (2)

SNAP-19 Power Generators Radioisotope Thermoelectric Generators

18-Nozzle Terminal Descent Engines (3)

Soil Sample Processors

Soil Sampler

NASA

Eleven months in space brought Viking I to within 348 000 miles of the surface of Mars (above) and to the final stages of its complicated journey. In July 1976, one year after the launch, the lander (right) touched down on the red planet to begin experimenting in its computerized 'laboratory'.

system and the processes which shaped the Earth, as well as to establish conditions on Mars.

The mechanical 'biology lab', housed in an unpretentious box the size of a large suitcase, was one of the most sophisticated pieces of scientific equipment ever created. It contained three automatic laboratories, a computer, tiny ovens, counters for radioactive tracers, filters, a sun lamp, a gas chromatograph to identify chemicals, 40 thermostats, 22 000 transistors, 18 000 other electronic parts and 43 miniature valves.

In the most exciting experiment of all—and the one which generated the most intense speculation—the lander scraped up samples of Martian soil with a mechanical scoop. The samples were then analyzed and tested for the simplest forms of life, or 'terrestrial bacteria'. It was the first real attempt to get close to that figment so beloved of science-fiction writers, the 'Little Green Men'.

For ever since the Italian astronomer Giovanni Schiaparelli reported a network of straight lines criss-crossing the surface of Mars a century ago, the possibility of life on the Red Planet has fascinated man. Spacecraft like Mariner 9, which went into orbit round Mars at the end of 1971 and sent back thousands of pictures, showed that Schiaparelli's 'canals' did not exist and that conditions on Mars were harsh in the extreme. But in spite of the Arctic cold, the thin atmosphere with its 200mph winds and the lack of liquid water, many of the hardier terrestrial micro-organisms could survive on Mars.

In one way, the earlier Mariner 9 pictures were encouraging as far as life on Mars was concerned. Life as we know it could not have appeared without liquid water, and liquid water cannot exist on Mars' surface; the atmosphere is too thin. But the Mariner pictures revealed a network of winding channels

showing all the signs of having been formed by flowing water. So there may have been water on Mars in the past, and in quantity.

Millions of years ago, conditions may have been less hostile to life and some robust forms may have survived. Dr. Michael McElroy of Harvard University, one of the team analyzing Viking's data, suggested that Mars may once have been stricken by catastrophic floods, with some of the water still frozen beneath the planet's surface. If there *were* any life, therefore, it could be underground.

And so Viking's amazing, telescopic arm reached out for the first samples of Martian soil. The spots covered by the arm—as much as ten feet from the lander—were selected by Earth-control after consulting the televised pictures. The arm scrabbled up a little soil with a

small scoop, retracted and swiveled, then deposited it in a hopper on top of the spacecraft. From there it was channeled to the 'life detection' equipment.

In one there-and-then experiment, a little soil was dropped into a mixture of organic chemicals on which Martian organisms might 'feed'. But this was a 'doctored diet' incorporating a radioactive form of carbon, Carbon-14. If 'Mars bugs' consumed the chemicals, they would convert some of the Carbon-14 to radioactive carbon dioxide which could be detected with a Geiger counter at the top of the experimental chamber.

Carbon-14 was used in a different way in another of the 'Is there life?' experiments. Here, the Martian soil was exposed to radioactive carbon dioxide and light at the same time, in the hope that if there were any organisms which could photosynthesize like plants on Earth, they would take some of it up. The Martian soil was then roasted. Any radioactive carbon dioxide given off at that stage would be a strong hint that there was indeed life on Mars.

The third Viking life-detection experiment measured the exchange of gases between any microbes in the soil and the atmosphere in the test chamber when a sample of Martian soil was incubated with several possible food-source chemicals. "Although no single test would

confirm life by itself," said rocket expert Wernher von Braun at the time, "a team of scientists should reach a pretty certain conclusion if all three pointed to living micro-organisms."

Despite initial scientific excitement at some of the chemical reactions, however, it was generally conceded later that no unequivocal signs of Martian life had been detected. This time, at least.

The mission which delivered this extraordinary active package to Mars began in August 1975 with the launch of the 6000-pound spacecraft on top of a Titan 3/Centaur rocket. First, Viking was propelled into a 'parking orbit' round the Earth. There it was in position for trans-Mars injection, accomplished with a 310-second burn of the liquid hydrogen-fuelled Centaur. This put Viking into a trajectory round the sun which would intercept Mars ten months later after a 'chase' of more than 500 million miles. Only a few minor course corrections had to be ordered from Earth to keep the spacecraft on target.

Scientific investigations actually began several days before Viking entered Mars' orbit. Its television cameras came on to take pictures of the planet's disc and infra-red detectors began scanning it, to map temperatures and water vapor in the atmosphere.

The thermal mapping instruments

worked by measuring the intensity of infra-red radiation from the surface of Mars at several different wavelengths. From these measurements, the temperature over the planet's disc was calculated. The information also helped to reveal the nature of the surface; for finely divided soil cools more quickly at night than large rocks.

Another detector was tuned to wavelengths in the infra-red range absorbed by water vapor. From variations in the intensity of this radiation as the instruments scanned the surface, it was possible to determine both the total amount of water in the atmosphere and to map its distribution.

If all the water in the Martian atmosphere fell out as rain it would probably amount to a fall of only a couple of thousandths of an inch—the equivalent figure for Earth is hundreds of times greater—but to scientists it was of enormous interest. For there were unexplained questions they wanted to know the answers to.

Does much water vapor escape into the atmosphere when one of the polar caps, which consist mainly of solid carbon dioxide, is shrinking? What has happened to all the hydrogen and oxygen that must have been present in the primeval matter from which Mars was formed about 4600 million years ago, if

11

Did a Martian leave this 'B' on a rock? People who phoned Viking control were told, "No, it's just a freak shadow effect."

it is not present in water? These were the questions Viking was taking the first steps to answer as it circled Mars.

Its television cameras, too, were hard at work before touchdown. They were searching for signs of volcanic activity below, and gathering information about the mysterious channels on the surface. The information flashed back to Earth would help scientists to work out how much water once flowed in them.

The cameras also played a vital part in what was technically the most difficult part of the mission: getting the lander safely onto the surface. They revealed that the site provisionally chosen for the landing was creased with channels and volcanic flows. Even a rock a yard across would have been enough to tip over the lander and wreck the whole mission.

The lander started making scientific observations in its own right as soon as it entered Mars' atmosphere, measuring the power of the electrically-charged upper regions and analyzing it with a miniature mass spectrometer.

The analysis showed that the Martian atmosphere contained small quantities of nitrogen, a gas not previously detected on the planet. Nitrogen is one of the essential chemicals for life—at least as we know it on Earth—and its discovery on Mars slightly increased the

chance of finding life there. The analysis also showed only a small quantity of argon, though indirect evidence from an earlier Russian probe had suggested that it might have been a major constituent of the Martian atmosphere: in large quantities, argon would have interfered with Viking's mass spectrometer gas analyzer.

Safely on Martian soil, Viking's great 'arsenal' of built-in observations and experiments could start. For Earth, the most immediate results were color stereoscopic pictures of the Martian landscape.

Viking's two cameras were spaced 39 inches apart and gauged to provide a panoramic view. The rotating cameras, containing 'nodding' mirrors, took 20 minutes to complete one 360° scan and although the pictures were only 'still life', their accuracy was so great they could view objects as small as a pea, even at close range. The cameras also included two improvements on the human eye: their stereo effect was greater and they could 'see' infra-red radiation beyond the range of sight.

On board the lander was a complete meteorological station for recording the Martian weather. It included wind gauges which depended on the rate at which the wind took heat away from projecting probes, thermocouples to measure temperatures and an aneroid barometer to measure atmospheric pressure. The day-to-day readings—although of compelling interest to scientists in building up a complete picture of

the weather on Mars—also provided one of Viking's few quirks of humor. After its first sol (as the Martian day of 24 hours and 36 minutes is called), Viking sent a 'weather forecast' which was quoted tongue-in-cheek in newspapers throughout the world. "It's a bright clear day on Mars this morning," was the chirpy message released by NASA. "The temperature at night will sink to about −127°F but will warm up to a more comfortable −5°F when the sun comes up again."

Although the lander 'blooped' in detecting Marsquakes—its three miniature seismometers in a six-inch cube failed to drop down—its other experiments were carried out perfectly, despite early trouble with the scoop arm. Meanwhile, its power unit was humming away to the delight of Earth scientists.

For Viking contained both a 'brain' and a 'heart'. Its computer brain, called the Guidance Control and Sequencing Computer, was specially designed. "An electronic wonder," was how one scientist described it.

The computer could do almost anything except sing Grand Opera. It could be re-programmed from Earth so that the spacecraft could respond to changing events, and also store information until it could be relayed back to Earth by the orbiter passing overhead.

Viking's own power—vital to keep instruments and heating apparatus working—came from radioactive thermoelectric generators. Heat produced by the radioactive decay of plutonium was converted directly into electricity. Earlier, scientists had rejected a solar powered system because sunlight is only half as strong on Mars as on Earth in the daylight and is non-existent during the freezing Martian night when the temperature can drop to −184°F.

Follow That!

Despite the enormous cost of the project, scientists were overjoyed at the results. Teams began to work on the data, assured that the final information would contribute immeasurably to mankind's knowledge of our solar system.

But before the final close-down Viking had one more task to perform; an interplanetary conjuring trick that seemed to say with smug satisfaction, 'Follow that!'

From 200 million miles away, Viking opened America's National Air and Space Museum, in Washington. Although the opening ceremony was performed by President Ford, it was Viking that did the work. At a signal from the spacecraft, radio waves activated a mechanical arm which cut the museum opening ribbon. The signal took just 18 minutes to reach Earth, opening not just a museum but a whole new era of space exploration.

EXORCISM PRELUDE TO MURDER

The man was terrified. He said the Devil was 'out to get him'. Despite grave misgivings, it was decided to employ the ritual of exorcism to rid his soul of tormenting spirits—like those which inflamed the nuns of Loudon. The result was the most appalling bloodbath.

The South American heat turned the interior of the little adobe hut into a clay oven, sending rivulets of dark sweat coursing under the woman's dress. The bed sheet was soaked, and an oily sheen highlighted her brown face, her breasts and bare legs.

There were two men in the room. They were both praying intensely, in unison. Each gripped a crucifix, and neither took his eyes for one instant from the woman. She was grotesquely arched in a sexual parody; only the back of her head and her heels touched the dirty sheet, while the rest of her body was flung upwards rigidly, unmoving.

"She had been like this for forty-eight hours," said the late Fr. Sam Farrell, an American Jesuit who was the younger of the two men. Writing home to Ohio, he continued, "She was the half-Indian widow of a Spanish doctor, who had worked on the mission station until six months previously, when he had died of a heart attack at forty years of age. Her grief had been extreme, but reserved. And now we had found her like this."

The Jesuit Father Rector of the little mission and school had had no time to consult his superiors. In the early period of her 'seizure' the woman, normally pious, had gurgled obscenities through clenched teeth. The year was 1923, and the works of Freud, Adler and Jung were virtually unknown in this part of the world. The Father Provincial had diagnosed 'possession' and had decided to perform an exorcism.

No Visible Means of Support

"As he recited the Doxology" (a short Roman Catholic prayer in praise of the trinity) "for the final time, an astounding thing happened. The woman rose up from the bed, with her heels as a pivot and without using her hands or any other part of her body. As she reached the upright position she threw herself across the room at me, with an absolutely animal shriek, and hurled me to the ground. I am over six feet tall . . . and I boxed at college, and she was about five three or four . . . but her strength was dreadful. She pinioned me by the shoulders like a wrestler and tried to take a bite from my throat."

Using all his strength, Fr. Farrell's companion held the woman's gaping mouth away from the fallen priest's jugular vein. And then, quite suddenly, the woman collapsed and lay sobbing quietly. The devil, or whatever it was, had left her. There was a curious sequel to the story. An hour before the final phase of the ritual, bread and fresh mutton had been brought into the hut for the priests, who had not eaten more than a mouthful of food during their vigil. When the woman had been laid back on the bed, and a nurse called, Fr.

Farrell turned to the food. The bread was already sprouting blue-green fungi, and the meat was slimy and corrupt.

Possibly the searing temperature had rotted the food, although, as Fr. Farrell remarked, the degree of decay was extraordinary for an hour's exposure. What the young Jesuit had learned, however, was the inherent physical and mental danger to an inexperienced priest in attempting an exorcism.

Sexual Hysteria

Today, psychiatrists would immediately recognize the woman's state as one of sexual hysteria, paralleled on many occasions in the Middle Ages and later in convents all over Europe, when nuns sporadically threw themselves about in erotic fits. One of the first recorded cases took place in a convent in Cambrai, France, in 1491, shortly after the appearance of the *Malleus maleficarum* or 'Hammer of Witches', a textbook for witch-hunters published by the Dominicans Kramer and Sprenger. One nun began barking like a dog, twisting herself into inhuman shapes and blaspheming; not unnaturally, in the closed atmosphere of the nunnery, she sparked off hysteria in her colleagues, and soon several of them were in the same state.

In the 16th century the Dutch physician Johannes Weyer made a small crack in the wall of lingering medieval superstition when he clinically observed a similar outbreak at the Nazareth Convent in Cologne, Germany. Here, the 'possessed' nuns behaved in a similar fashion to Fr. Farrell's patient, thrusting their bodies forward in a suggestive way, though Dr. Weyer did remark that even as they were doing it, their eyes "were . . . opened with apparent expressions of shame and pain."

The Dutchman investigated further and discovered that the outbreak had started when a young nun had secretly taken a lover from the local village. He was followed by others, who for a while had carried on clandestine affairs with a number of the convent inmates. When these visits suddenly stopped, the hysteria began, induced, perhaps, by intense guilt and shame.

Dr. Weyer was ferociously attacked by the Church establishment, but held his ground. Despite the fact that he believed to a certain extent in the objective existence of demons, he used his observations in Cologne as part of the basis for an attack on indiscriminate witch-hunting, published in 1563 as the classic *De Praestigiis Daemonum*. His words echo modern critics of indiscriminate exorcism: "The uninformed and unskilled physicians relegate all the incurable diseases, or all the diseases the remedy for which they overlook, to witchcraft. In all

such cases a good doctor is to be consulted because nothing is more important than to make the clinical situations as clear as daylight, for in no domain of human life are human passions so freely at play as in this one, these passions being superstition, rage, hate, and malice."

Despite Dr. Weyer's sound common sense, the outbreaks, and their attendant 'exorcisms' accompanied by torture and death, continued: at Oldham on Rhine in 1577, where over-excited dogs were said to have attacked the nuns; at Milan in 1599, where the convent was invaded by incubi—male sex demons; and at Lille in 1613, where a similar occult invasion occurred.

In the two most famous cases, those at Aix in 1609 and Loudon in 1634, the depravity of the nuns possessed was equalled and even surpassed by the brutality of their 'exorcists'. Both cases began with a few oversexed women, whose fits heightened the feeling of sexual frustration in the convent, and led to mass hysteria. Each case caused the downfall of local priests who were guilty of no more than, perhaps, stupidity.

At Aix, the prime mover was a pretty young nymphomaniac named Madeleine de Mandol, who was supposedly possessed by a demon named Verrine. 'Verrine' told the exorcists that the town's pastor, Louis Gaufridi, was magically 'attacking' the nuns. While Madeleine and her colleagues were given painful enemas and douches, the ritual of exorcism was read over them, and Gaufridi was tortured, strangled, and burned to ashes.

The Devils

In the famous Loudon case, filmed as *The Devils*, the principal nun was Sister Jeanne des Anges, the 25-year-old Mother Superior of an Ursuline convent. She formed an obsessive attachment for a rakish young priest named Urbain Grandier, who had been foolish enough to have open 'affairs' in the town. When Grandier refused to become confessor for the convent—perhaps suspecting that Sister Jeanne might stir up trouble—the Mother Superior began to have the characteristic sexual fits, as did many of her sisters. The 'exorcists' moved in, hideously tortured Grandier and finally burned him alive. But the 'possessions' continued for some time afterwards, only fading out after rather more rational exorcisms had been performed by a Jesuit named Surin.

In all these cases—leaving aside the savagery of the 'treatment'—a purely psychological element was involved which 'normal' exorcism failed to combat; in many cases the exorcism did positive harm, as few of the nuns appear ever to have returned to a stable state of mind. Sister Jeanne des Anges, for in-

stance, became almost manically pious. What alarms the modern medical profession is that exorcism is being used to treat similar cases today—sometimes without reference to psychiatry first.

When a popular London Sunday newspaper conducted a survey among exorcism patients in the 1970s they discovered that the majority were women, mainly adolescent girls whose 'crush' on pop-singing idols had reached the point of mania, or middle-aged, frustrated housewives. Each group—as a psychiatrist pointed out—cases for medical, rather than spiritual, treatment.

Loudon and Aix are not far from us emotionally, according to Sir Martin Roth, President of the Royal College of Psychiatrists.

In a statement to the London *Sunday Times,* he said that he felt a real danger of 'spirit possession spreading by contagion' in the modern Western world, exactly as it did in the convents of medieval Europe. "One person screaming hysterically can set off another. Exorcism is an impressive ritual which could have seriously disturbing and dangerous effects on some people. The experience could terrify a patient whose links with reality are already tenuous and bring to the surface reactions the person cannot control. There is a danger of violence when a psychotic illness is stirred up."

Perhaps the medical man with most specialized knowledge of possession—he made a personal study of Voodoo trance states in the West Indies—is Dr. William Sargant, consultant psychiatrist at St. Thomas's Hospital, London, and author of such books as *Battle for the Mind* and *The Mind Possessed.* In an

interview with the London *Times,* Dr. Sargant described an exorcism he had watched. "One man who came from Yorkshire was a schizophrenic," he said. "He claimed that for five years voices had been telling him to kill himself. It is dangerous to meddle with such people because the voices might start to tell him to kill someone else."

Dr. Sargant had observed that exorcism 'patients' often went into what was

There were three demons that never left Michael Taylor (above left) even after his exorcism by Rev. Peter Vincent. After this nightlong ordeal—with the forces of 'murder', 'violence' and 'insanity' still in him—he went home and brutally murdered his wife.

virtually an hypnotic trance when exorcized. If a person in that condition is told, for instance, that he has the spirit of a murderer within him, he may well believe it and go out and kill someone. According to Dr. Sargant, 'normal' people are unlikely to do things under hypnosis which would be objectionable to them, but this is not so with the mentally unbalanced. They are subject to a 'much wider range of suggestion'.

Like his colleagues, Dr. Sargant is convinced that the Western world is now ripe for an epidemic of spirit possession. "There is an increasing interest in the supernatural because the Church has failed. The Church of England, and the Methodists too, are dying on their feet because the Church service does not relieve emotion. The approach is too intellectual. Too many Anglican bishops have double firsts at Cambridge. There could be an epidemic of religious fervor, as there was in Wesley's time, with clergymen preaching hell fire and damnation or some modern equivalent. But the danger is that once people lose faith they are open to influence by other gods which may not be so benevolent."

And this certainly seems to have been the case in Britain and America. The

15

occult revival of the 60s and 70s, during which thousands of people turned to such esoteric pursuits as witchcraft, satanism, necromancy and apparently harmless practices like table-turning and tarot reading, has led to many suitable cases for exorcism. In such cases, psychiatrists agree, exorcism may prove successful as part of therapy, in conjunction with orthodox medical treatment.

A leading Catholic doctor explained: "You see, whether you believe in demonic possession or not to begin with, you are laying yourself open to all manner of influences in a witchcraft or satanist group. An unstable person—who may only be joining for company and curiosity—can soon be whipped into a trance by the dancing, ritual, and so on. Soon he may come to believe that magical powers do exist—and when he tries to leave the coven he becomes convinced that these powers are arrayed against him. Orthodox hypnotism and counter-suggestion may work, but as the fears are emotional and spiritual to begin with, they are often best met by means of the emotional and spiritual power of the exorcism ritual."

One of the few psychiatrists who readily admits to using exorcism regularly is Dr. R. K. McCall, who spent 12 years as a medical missionary in China and is now practicing in Hampshire, England. "A mass of people in mental hospitals all over the country would benefit from exorcism," Dr. McCall states. A religious man, Dr. McCall found that in certain cases prayer was helpful to his patients. A clergyman friend then suggested he try exorcism for more stubborn traumas of a religious nature. As a result, Dr. McCall has referred about 200 people to Roman Catholic, Church of England, Methodist or Jewish clergymen for exorcism over the last 16 years.

According to him, exorcism can "cure mental illness even if the patient does not participate." He claims that on one occasion he attended a ritual performed outside a padded cell, in which the afflicted person was raging. "The patient suddenly quietened at the appropriate moment," said Dr. McCall, "he was completely cured."

Lord's Prayer

As a Christian, Dr. McCall often uses a mild form of exorcism himself while actually treating mental illness. The Lord's Prayer, he claims, is the simplest form and, said meaningfully, can be used by anyone. "Sometimes I just tell Satan I have spotted him and he can mind his own business. I tell him to buzz off in the name of Jesus Christ."

A full exorcism as recommended by the Bishop of Exeter's report is a much more impressive affair, capable of generating very powerful emotions —either for good or ill, depending on the personal point of view. The report suggests that only 'mature Christian people who are sympathetic to the ministry' should be present, with, if possible, a doctor and a psychiatrist. If a woman is to be dealt with, then at least one other woman should attend. Two exorcists are preferred to one, in case doubt and extreme fear attack one of them, and if the exorcism takes place in a house, animals and children should be taken away and the latter given a prayer of protection before the service begins.

In the prayer for personal exorcism the form suggested reads: "The Exorcist, standing before the patient, shall say: 'I command you, every evil spirit, in the name of God the Father Almighty, in the name of Jesus Christ his only Son and in the name of the Holy Spirit that, harming no one, you depart from this creature of God, and return to the place appointed you; there to remain for ever'."

Both skeptic and believer might be forgiven for thinking that the whole question of exorcism has, in the past few years, been exaggerated out of all proportion by the media and in particularly by such films as *The Exorcist*. Unfortunately, in September 1974, a tragedy occurred in the little Yorkshire town of Ossett, near Wakefield, which proved the literal truth of the warnings given by Sir Martin Roth and Dr. Sargant.

Murder Under the Influence

A 31-year-old man, described by his neighbors as a 'loving and devoted husband and father', went to be exorcized, and immediately returned home to tear his wife to death with his bare hands.

Michael Taylor and his 29-year-old wife Christine had five young sons. She was described in court as the 'darling of his life'. In the late summer of 1974, Taylor began attending meetings of the Christian Fellowship Group, which gathered for Bible reading and hymn singing, while Christine and the children stayed at home. One evening Taylor came back in a 'shaken condition'. He told his mother that he had seen the devil while the hymns were being sung and the prayers read; he swore that the vision had been 'real' and that the devil was out to 'get' him.

It was a period when the publicity for exorcism was at its peak and when Taylor visited the Rev. Peter Vincent, vicar of St. Thomas's church in Barnsley, the Anglican minister decided to try the ancient ceremony. The vicar's wife said that 'there was an enormous force of evil' emanating from Taylor, and that only a long and arduous ceremony would rid him of his supernatural problems. Two local Methodists, the Rev. Raymond Smith and lay preacher Donald James, were summoned, and although Smith claimed 'he had had word from God that Taylor needed psychiatric treatment', he was overruled.

At the subsequent trial, the prosecuting attorney, Geoffrey Barker, QC, was to tell how Taylor was taken to the vestry of St. Thomas's at midnight, and laid out on hassocks on the floor. At times he had to be held down, while 'they took it in turns to exorcize each particular demon as it was called out'.

40 or 50 Demons

A list was made of '40 or 50' of these demons, including evil spirits governing incest, bestiality, blasphemy, heresy, lewdness and masochism. By 6.00 the following morning all the participants were exhausted; Mrs. Vincent, who seems to have acted as a sort of devil detector, claimed that only three entities were left in Taylor's body—those of insanity, murder, and violence. Smith had previously said that God had suggested medical care for Taylor, and now Mrs. Smith said that she had had word from God that Taylor, if allowed to go home, would murder his wife.

An effort was made to call a welfare officer, but it was too early in the morning; none was available. Finally the Taylors, Michael and Christine, were driven home, and shortly afterwards Michael turned on his wife, throttled her, and tore out her eyes and tongue.

His trial, in March 1975, lasted only three hours. He had spent the previous four months in Broadmoor, an institution for the criminally insane, but had been adjudged fit to plead. He pleaded not guilty, and Leeds Crown Court found that he was not guilty 'by reason of insanity' and he was sent back to Broadmoor for an indefinite period.

Geoffrey Barker said that all the people who had taken part in the botched exorcism shared the moral responsibility for the unspeakably brutal murder, and police evidence pathetically bore this out. After killing his wife, and strangling her mother's poodle, Taylor had walked the streets of Ossett naked, his hair, face and body smeared with drying blood, his wife's gold rings on his fingers.

At 10.45 am the police found him. He was on his hands and knees with his forehead touching the ground, motionless. An officer asked him where the blood came from, and he said, "It is the blood of Satan."

Michael Taylor told the police, "I have killed my wife. I know I have. It came through religion. They primed me for this last night. They tried to bring me peace of mind. But instead they filled me with the devil."

The Devil which exorcism or modern psychiatry, applied with care and understanding, can cast out.

THEY STROLLED THROUGH A HOLE IN TIME

Men in strange uniforms hurried past. People spoke to them in French. Women wore old-fashioned dress and 18th-century music drifted on the air. There was no doubt that the two women were walking in pre-Revolution France. What was astounding·was that the year was 1901 . . . more than 100 years further on in history.

Mansell

When two English women toured Versailles they were visiting history —with a difference. Where the formal avenues gave way to a 'wilderness' (right of picture), they met guards in archaic costume and a man uncannily like the Comte de Vaudreil (right) who had been dead 100 years.

The heat in Paris on the afternoon of August 10, 1901, was oppressive and the two English 'bluestockings' decided the most sensible thing to do was to visit the Palace of Versailles and its extensive grounds for a breath of fresh country air.

What happened to them then provided the world with one of the greatest-ever mysteries of the supernatural.

For—unwittingly, at first—the two women found themselves transported back in time to the days of Marie-Antoinette and the French Revolution. Instead of taking a conventional stroll, they walked back more than 100 years into another period in history.

What makes their story doubly incredible is the character of the two women; both intelligent and with an academic background. Neither was the kind to

risk ridicule or tarnish their undoubtedly serious reputations by fabricating a bizarre tale.

The two women, both spinsters and prominent figures in the world of education, were Charlotte Moberly, daughter of a former Bishop of Salisbury, and Eleanor Jourdain, whose intellectual enthusiasms ranged from classical drama to philosophy. Miss Moberly was already principal of St Hugh's Hall, the newly-created Oxford college for women. Miss Jourdain, author of a scholarly study on *The Theory of the Infinite in Modern Thought*, was to succeed her when she retired many years after their historic adventure.

No sooner had the ladies arrived at Versailles than they lost their way, with the result that they eventually approached the area of the palace grounds

called the Petit Trianon by a little-used path. As they rounded some outbuildings at the end of the Petit Trianon garden, both were gripped by a curious feeling of depression, but neither remarked on the fact. "We were afraid of spoiling the afternoon out," both explained later.

When they reached the Flower Garden, the path they were following forked into three and they puzzled over which route to take. Fortunately, two men wearing uniforms and cloaks were standing nearby, engaged in conversation. The two friends asked them which path they should follow to reach the Maison, the house which had once been the home of the ill-fated Marie-Antoinette. "Straight on," said one of the men.

Eventually they came to a small kiosk, shaped like a bandstand. In the shade of the trees around it sat a swarthy man with a scarred face, who was wrapped in a cloak and wore a sombrero hat. The path forked around the kiosk and, as they again hesitated over which direction to take, they heard running footsteps behind them and the call *"Mesdames, mesdames!"* The voice was that

Mary Evans

Hulton Picture Library

of a young man, also wearing a cloak and sombrero, who proceeded to tell them "The righthand fork will take you to the Maison."

Following his instructions, they crossed a small rustic bridge, and proceeded along a path heavily overhung with trees. Eventually they found another path which led them to the Maison where, with one exception, all the windows were shuttered. Miss Moberly heard a door bang and a servant appeared along the terrace. He told them that the entrance to the house was on the far side, which could be reached through the Cour d'Honneur—below the west terrace on which they were standing—and the French Garden. Then he hustled them on their way.

Yet, in terms of our ordinary experience, none of this could have happened. The men the spinsters claimed to have seen, and in some cases spoken to, were not alive in August 1901, and most of the physical features mentioned in their story had also long ceased to exist.

Once inside the Maison the two women were joined by a chattering throng of French tourists and taken on a conventional conducted tour of the house. At this stage both felt there had been something very peculiar about their walk through the Petit Trianon grounds and gardens, but, astonishingly, they kept their thoughts to themselves. It was not until a week later when Miss Moberly, writing to a friend about the visit, was suddenly gripped again by the feeling of depression she had first experienced on rounding the outbuildings; and she was prompted to ask her companion, "Do you think the Petit Trianon is haunted?"

Ghostly Guards

Miss Jourdain had no doubts. "Yes, I do," she said.

They talked the matter over. Both were convinced, it transpired, that The Guards, the first two men they had encountered, must have been ghosts because their greenish-gray uniforms and three-cornered hats seemed to belong to another age. At this time, however, they did not have any suspicions about the other men they had met although they did talk briefly about The Man By The Kiosk and The Running Man, both of whom had worn cloaks and sombreros. "Perhaps they were on their way to fight a duel," suggested Miss Moberly.

They did not discuss the matter again until three months later when, on November 10, Miss Jourdain visited Miss Moberly at her Oxford college. In the course of the conversation Miss Moberly asked: "What did you think of the lady sketching by the terrace?"

"I didn't see any lady sketching by the terrace," replied Miss Jourdain.

Miss Moberly was surprised because she had observed the lady distinctly, and they had both, in fact, passed quite close to her. With a sober regard for the truth, which characterized all their researches over the next decade, the two women decided not to mull over the details of their Versailles visit any more but that each of them would write an independent account of all they could remember about it.

Miss Moberly included an extremely detailed description of The Lady's appearance: "She had on a shady, white hat, perched on a good deal of fair hair that fluffed round her forehead. Her light summer dress was arranged on her shoulders in handkerchief fashion, and there was a little line of either green or

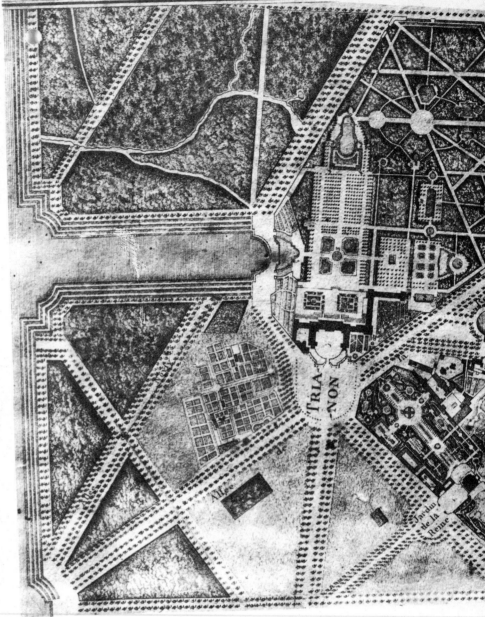

gold near the edge of the handkerchief, which showed me that it was *over*, not tucked into, her bodice, which was cut low. Her dress was long-waisted, with a good deal of fullness in the skirt, which seemed to be short. I thought she was a tourist, but that her dress was old-fashioned and rather unusual (though people were wearing *fichu* bodices that summer) . . . her *fichu* was pale green."

Miss Jourdain's account did not mention The Lady but contained some details missing from Miss Moberly's. While taking directions from The Guards she had noticed a cottage to her right. A woman was at the door, handing a jug to a young girl standing below her on some stone steps. By the Petit Trianon outbuildings she had seen some farm implements, including a plough.

While the two women were preparing their independent accounts, a new ele-

ment entered the story. While giving a history lesson, Miss Jourdain realized that August 10, the date of their visit to Versailles, had a special significance. August 10, 1792, was the date that the French monarchy was overturned. On that day King Louis XVI and his queen, Marie-Antoinette, began the imprisonment which would end with both their deaths by guillotine. On discussing this curious coincidence with friends, she learned that there was a tradition that the Queen and members of her court could still sometimes be seen in the Petit Trianon grounds on or about that anniversary. In fact the Royal Family had not lived at Versailles since October 1789, the year the Revolution began, so, as the other evidence suggests that it was to 1789 that the ladies were transported, the 'anniversary' appears to be something of a red herring.

It was decided that, during the Christmas vacation, Miss Jourdain should return to Paris and make another visit to the Petit Trianon. She went out to Versailles on January 2 and began her investigations by trying to find that kiosk. There was no trace of it anywhere. Then she suddenly found herself the victim of another odd and frightening experience, accompanied by the familiar feeling of depression.

In an open glade, she saw two men in capes loading a cart with sticks. Shortly afterwards, she wandered into a wood where another cloaked man appeared briefly before vanishing into the undergrowth. Although it was January she could hear the rustle of silk all around her and murmurs of *"Monsieur"* and *"Madame."* The sound of light music drifted on the winter air. Miss Jourdain made several attempts to escape from

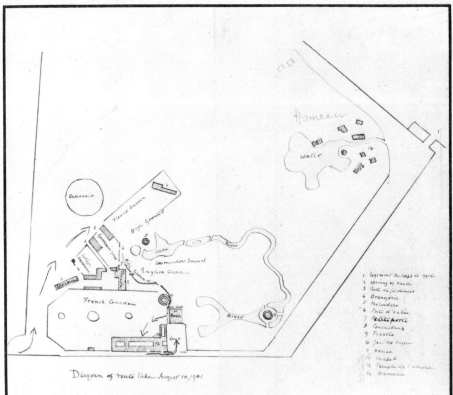

Diagram of route taken August 10, 1901

One of the privileged pair sits pondering her time-trip to Versailles. The ladies were haunted by their experience, making copious notes—among which is a hand-drawn map of their route. It tallies precisely with the area around Jardin de la Reine on this pre-Revolution map.

the wood, only to lose her way each time, until a tall gardener appeared and guided her. Then she returned to Paris where she wrote down a dozen bars of the music she had heard.

The absence of the kiosk, and the second appearance of ghostly figures, voices and music, led the two friends to decide to return to Versailles together at the first opportunity. This did not occur until the summer of 1904. On July 9 they set out for the Petit Trianon to try to retrace the route they had taken in 1901. They found it impossible.

They could not find the three paths where they had seen The Guards. They could not find the cottage with the stone steps, the kiosk or the rustic bridge. Exactly where The Lady had been sketching was a large bush which had clearly been growing there for several years. There was no terrace where the

door had slammed and The Servant appeared. Nor was there any trace of the wood in which Miss Jourdain had lost herself on her second visit.

This 1904 journey was the first of several joint expeditions, all of which failed to locate the features they remembered so distinctly. Miss Jourdain, however, had yet a third odd experience on September 12, 1908, when she had gone to Versailles alone to take some photographs. She had just come across two women, dressed in modern clothes and engaged in a heated argument, when . . .

" . . . suddenly, and utterly unexpectedly, I knew that some indefinable change had taken place. I felt as though I were being taken up into another condition of things quite as real as the former. The women's voices, though their quarrel was just as shrill and eager as before, seemed to be fading so quickly away that they would soon be gone altogether; from their tones, the dispute was clearly still going on, but seemed to have less and less power to reach me.

"I turned at once to look back, and saw the gates near which they were sitting melting away, and the background of

trees again becoming visible through them as on our original visit. The whole scene—sky, trees and buildings—gave a little shiver, like the movement of a curtain or of scenery as at a theater. At the same time, the old difficulty of walking on and making any way reproduced itself, together with the feeling of depression described in 1901 and 1902. But I instantly decided to keep to my plan of going straight out by the lane, and once outside the lane, things became natural again."

Between these intermittent visits the two friends also delved into some odd corners of history with some extraordinary results, finally revealed in 1911 when, under assumed names and the modest title *An Adventure*, they published an account of their experiences and the fruits of their research.

Dressmaker to the Queen

Among the sources they had consulted in an attempt to establish the identity of The Lady was the *Journal* of Madame Eloffe, dressmaker to Marie-Antoinette.

This disclosed that the Queen had frequently worn the kind of clothing described by Miss Moberly and also contained the entry: "During the year 1789 . . . Mme. Eloffe repaired several light, washing, short skirts, and made, in July and September, two green silk bodices, besides many large *fichus*."

From other documents they established that the bush, growing on the exact spot where The Lady was seen sketching, had been planted in the 19th

On their unnerving visit to Versailles in 1901 the ladies had seen a 'kiosk' ... which they could never find again. Later they compared a sketch they had made (top) with details of a *Ruine* that had stood in that place during the reign of Louis XVI.

landscape gardener to the queen, showed the presence of a cottage, with stone steps leading up to it, and Miss Moberly and Miss Jourdain came to the conclusion that The Girl being handed the jug of water could have been one of Marie-Antoinette's protegées, who later married Charpentier, the head gardener.

It had also emerged from their research that the cape and sombrero were common apparel for gentlemen in the last years before the Revolution, and they thought it likely that The Man By The Kiosk, dark-skinned with a scarred face, was the Comte de Vaudreuil, a "pock-marked Creole" who was one of the Queen's attendants.

The terrace along which The Servant approached them had existed in Marie-Antoinette's time although it had been demolished by 1901. There was also evidence of a construction to match their kiosk, which they had described in more detail as "a building with some columns roofed in." It was a *Ruine* with seven ionic columns and a domed roof, designed by Mique and built in 1787. A Mique map of the gardens, drawn at the time, also showed the wood with many paths into which Miss Jourdain had strayed on her second visit.

Idiom of the Past

Without revealing their significance, Miss Jourdain had also shown a French musical expert the bars of music she wrote down on her return to Paris after that second visit. He came to the conclusion that "the bars could hardly all belong to one another, but the idiom dates from about 1780." After subsequently hearing her story, he suggested Sacchini as the possible composer.

Miss Moberly and Miss Jourdain are now both dead. Their original statements and Miss Jourdain's notebooks recording the progress of their 10 years of research and investigation are, however, preserved in the Bodleian Library at Oxford.

It is difficult to imagine these two distinguished figures in the world of learning concocting an elaborate hoax over tea and crumpets in Oxford; doing all the research; faking the initial incident; devoting 10 years to repeating the research, visiting Versailles and faking two more incidents; publishing a book under assumed names; and finally depositing the written evidence with one of Britain's leading libraries for the benefit of posterity.

Critics, of course, have tried—without much success—to take their story to pieces. But, whatever the explanation, one thing is certain: Miss Moberly and Miss Jourdain went to their graves still convinced that, on that hot afternoon in 1901, they found themselves strolling in pre-Revolutionary France.

century. They should therefore have seen the bush, not The Lady, in 1901. Evidence also came to light that King Louis XV had bought a plough which was kept at Versailles and used sometimes for amusement by his grandson, the Dauphin. There was even a portrait of the Dauphin ploughing.

It was also clear that The Guards whom they asked for directions on their first visit could not have been either officials or gardeners. In 1901, officials wore black coats and white trousers while gardeners wore rough jerseys and round caps. On the other hand, Miss Jourdain and Miss Moberly, with the aid of an expert in military uniforms, had been able to identify the greenish-gray clothing of The Guards as the uniform of the *Gardes Suisses*, on duty whenever Marie-Antoinette was in residence.

The evidence did not end there. The memoirs of the Comte d'Hezecques, who visited the Trianon gardens in the 1780s, describe a kind of mini-Switzerland which existed there at that time, complete with pine trees and a little rustic bridge. A map by Mique,

KISS OF DEATH

The young couple in the nightclub only wanted a little privacy to kiss and cuddle. So the man removed a light-bulb from among the artificial palm fronds. His simple action was to lead to a disaster claiming nearly 500 victims, allegations of official negligence and the trial of a man who put greed before human life.

The Boston Sunday Globe EXTRA!

400 DEAD IN HUB NIGHT CLUB FIRE

Hundreds Hurt in Panic as the Cocoanut Grove Becomes Wild Inferno

By SAMUEL B. CUTLER

It was mid-evening at the Cocoanut Grove, the most popular and exclusive nightspot in Boston, Mass. A jampacked crowd was laughing and dancing and flirting. A piano was jingling a catchy ragtime tune, though almost swamped by the babble of voices and the clink of glasses.

Minutes later, a horde of hysterical women, their hair and clothes already smouldering, were trying to claw and elbow their way out of an inferno. The whole place was ablaze.

Incredibly, a huge and determined man was trying to force them back. In the heat and acrid blackness behind them were hundreds of other desperate people—choking and stumbling over the dead and the dying. Still the big man, guarding one of the few doorways to safety, was resolutely blocking their path. He had his orders, and he was sticking to them. "Nobody gets out!" he was shouting. "Not without paying his bill!"

The mob, crazed with terror, crushed him to the ground and trampled over him. Many of them reached the street, but died later in hospital.

That bizarre incident was typical of the stupidity and the vicious avarice that culminated in the great Boston disaster. A total of 492 people died on Saturday, November 28, 1942, when fire engulfed the Cocoanut Grove with terrifying suddenness. Another 181 were injured, many to be crippled or scarred for the rest of their lives.

The Fatal Cuddle

And all because a young man wanted to cuddle his girl-friend in privacy. All he did was to remove a low-powered light bulb . . . an apparently innocent action which was to have catastrophic results.

But, more than anything, the dead were victims of greed; the greed of a racketeer called Barney Welansky, who owned the Cocoanut Grove. His cynical disregard for all the rules of safety made him the chief culprit and he was given a prison sentence.

Nor did the authorities emerge with much credit from that frightful night. The people of Boston were to be appalled at revelations of official negligence.

The Cocoanut Grove, with its artificial palm trees and garish murals of tropical lagoons, was the regular rendezvous for socialites and top business executives. They never suspected—until the scandal broke—that they were drinking contraband liquor. Or that, in patronizing the club, they were risking their lives.

Overcrowded

On that November night, as on so many earlier occasions, nearly 1000 people were packed into the Cocoanut Grove. One of them was a police captain who later said he was there merely to make a routine check. He agreed, however, that he had not protested about the illegal overcrowding.

Outside, as usual, the multicolored neons were winking their insistent invitation, "*Dance and Dine at the Cocoanut Grove . . . Visit the Melody Lounge.*"

Inside, there were scenes of unusually wild festivity. A football team called Holy Cross had just trounced the previously undefeated Boston College. And, in the main lounge, a large crowd of Holy Cross supporters were noisily celebrating the unexpected triumph.

Veteran Hollywood cowboy Buck Jones, exhausted after traveling the

After the holocaust came the post mortem. Stanley Tomaszewski (top), the young employee who lit the fatal match, gives evidence before the Grand Jury, set up to establish the cause of the nightclub inferno. Barney Welansky (right), owner and manager, was found guilty of manslaughter through his criminal negligence and sentenced to 12-15 years in jail. The investigations also revealed his other criminal enterprises, such as selling illicit liquor at the club.

country on a stint of selling War Bonds, was relaxing in another part of the lounge with a party of friends.

Down below, in the dimly lit Melody Lounge, a young man in a dinner-jacket was cuddling his girlfriend. No one paid any attention to them. They were just a couple of kids having fun`. . .

It was 10 p.m. and time for the floor-show. Compere Billy Payne left his table, all ready to go into his 'hello-hello-and-welcome' routine, when band-leader Mickey Alpert signaled to him with a shake of the head. The waiters were still scurrying busily and they needed a few minutes before the show could start. Payne went back to his seat.

The young man in the Melody Lounge whispered to his girl. She giggled and

nodded. He removed an electric-light bulb from its shade of cocoanut husk. That gave them a little more privacy. The time was 10.5 p.m.

An assistant waiter, 16-year-old Stanley Tomaszewski, was ordered to replace the light bulb. He climbed on a settee to do so but could not find the socket because of the thick artificial palm fronds. It was then 10.11 p.m.

Tomaszewski struck a match to see what he was doing. The fronds, like all the decorations in the club, were highly inflammable. The time was exactly 10.12 p.m.

There was a crackling noise as vivid red flames flared up the fronds and started licking at the ceiling of the Melody Lounge.

being filled with thick and choking smoke.

Her fiancé, who had stayed to settle the bill, was among those who never got out alive.

Still the club was getting more crowded. People were surging in through the revolving doors under the neon signs when the first gust of smoke started billowing up from the Melody Lounge and into the thickly carpeted foyer. Within seconds the Cocoanut Grove was a blazing shambles. Furniture was smashed as the screaming crowds started to stampede to safety.

Journalist Martin Sheridan, who was a member of the Buck Jones party, was just finishing an oyster cocktail when he heard the first warning shout. The word being shouted was 'fire' but he thought it was 'fight'. He said later, "Liquor had been flowing freely among the supporters of the rival football clubs and I assumed a brawl had broken out."

Then the black smoke began to gush into the main lounge. The noise of the blaze was getting louder and the heat was coming up through the floor.

Some of the more level-headed men were desperately trying to stop the panic. "Don't rush," they were shouting. "For God's sake don't rush. Just take it easy to the nearest exit." But where were the exits? People were floundering around trying to find them.

Joyce Spector, sitting with her fiancé in the 40-foot square room, thought of her new $750 leopard-skin coat. It was upstairs in the clockroom and she wanted to make sure it came to no harm. She said quietly to her fiancé, "I'll go get my coat and we'll leave."

There was a ladies' powder room at the top of the stairs and, as she passed, she poked her head into it. "Hey, girls —there's a little fire downstairs," she said. "Don't get excited but you'd better start getting out."

She did not realize that by then it was no longer a little fire. The fire had swept with sudden ferocity among the varnished palms and blazing fragments were dropping on the diners and the drinkers in the lounge. The room was

One of the lucky ones: one woman is carried to safety, though she does not yet know how many of her dinner party were among the 492 people killed in the fire.

Martin Sheridan recalled, "The exits were not identified or illuminated. There were no signs like they have in cinemas. I took a couple of steps. Then I began to choke from the poisonous fumes which swept through the place. I felt myself sinking slowly to the floor, falling on the people in front of me. The last things I remember were people screaming and the crash and clatter from breaking dishes and glasses and overturned tables. The world caved in on me in a matter of seconds."

He was dragged clear. His injuries were so severe that a priest gave him the last rites before he was taken to hospital. But Martin Sheridan was among the lucky ones . . .

Locked Exits

Welansky's contempt for the law sealed the fate of hundreds of his clients. A wall had been built in front of one emergency exit. Another exit, in defiance of all regulations, was locked and barred.

The scrummage was so savage at the main revolving door that it jammed, held rigid by the weight of the bodies wedged against it and trapped in it. People at the front, seeing they could not possibly escape that way, tried to fight their way back in—hoping to find another escape route—and they were battling against those still blindly trying to reach the door.

Nearly 200 people died near that door. People outside, hearing their screams, were trying to batter their way in. And each time a window was shattered the smoke and flames belched out into the street.

Then all the lights failed. There was no secondary emergency power system. Welansky, in his usual cut-cost style, had arranged for all his electrical work to be done on the cheap—by unlicensed workmen and without a city permit.

Leopard-skin Coat

Joyce Spector, her leopard-skin coat forgotten, had been knocked to the floor when panic had exploded in the main lounge. She had crawled through the filth and the blackness, picking her way over and around the writhing bodies, until she had felt fresh air on her face.

She was safe. Then a weight fell on her. A man had stumbled from the blazing building and had collapsed, dead, on top of her. The terror and the effort had brought on his final heart attack.

The club's cashier, middle-aged Katharine Swett, was one of the first to escape. She was trembling with shock as rescue workers tried to comfort her. Suddenly she broke free from them and, before they could stop her, she darted back into the building. "The money!" she

was explaining frantically. "I must save the money!" Her charred body, scarcely identifiable, was later found beside a cash box. It contained $2000.

While Katharine Swett was running back to her death, passing motorists were being flagged down and asked to give blood. Local hospitals, although highly efficient, did not have enough

The bar and its surrounds went up like tinder, as guests fled in panic, looking for exits that did not exist. No one ever tried to re-open the ill-fated club; the charred remains of furniture stood untouched as a memorial to those who were burned to death . . . until the club was flattened to make a car park.

emergency supplies to cope with a disaster on this scale.

Cars and taxis were being commandeered to take the injured to hospital and the dead to makeshift mortuaries. So were post-office trucks and delivery vans.

Victims were being shunted into Boston City Hospital at the rate of one every 11 seconds—faster than the numbers going into any single London hospital at the height of the Nazi air-raids of World War Two. One of those victims was Buck Jones, who died there.

Joyce Spector and young Stanley Tomaszewski—the waiter who had struck the fatal match—were among those whose lives were saved.

Refuge in the Fridge

Meanwhile, back in the Cocoanut Grove, the living were still trapped with the dead. They were still struggling, against all odds, for survival.

One man grabbed his wife's wrist in the darkness. If they were to die, they would at least die together. The pair of them crawled blindly into a downstairs kitchen.

They bumped into something solid and his hand, groping upwards, touched what felt like a wooden handle. He pulled on it to help himself up and heard a voice say, "Jump in quick. This is the refrigerator. It's fireproof."

The three of them—the man, his wife and the stranger—were still there, alive, when the firemen eventually reached them.

Upstairs, in the chorus-girls' dressing-room, a group of girls—wearing their scanty spangled costumes—had been playing cards while waiting to make their entrance. They were only vaguely aware that something was wrong—until 19-year-old dancer Marshall Cook burst in on them. "Quick! Out of the window and on to the roof!" he shouted. "There's no other way!"

They followed him and escaped across the roof of the adjoining buildings. Other girls, one wearing nothing under her fur coat, jumped from lower windows and were caught by rescue workers below.

Others were not so fortunate as they tried to reach safety through the windows.

Human Torch

One elderly man took off his shoe and used it to smash a hole in a window of glass bricks. He managed to make a gap barely big enough for him to wriggle through. He was halfway through it when his entire body was enveloped in a great belch of flame. Firemen were unable to reach him as he hung there, screaming, with his clothing and flesh disintegrating in the intense heat.

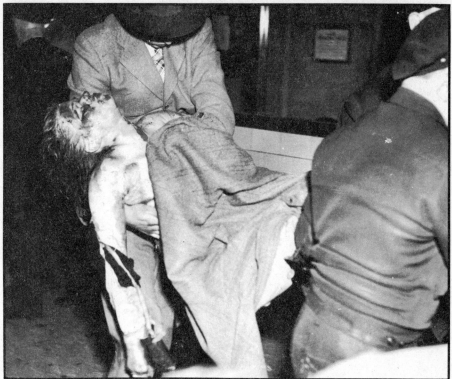

At a nearby window a younger man hesitated before he jumped. His foot slipped as he threw himself from the ledge and he pitched forward awkwardly. His back was broken as he hit the road.

And every moment the guilt of Barney Welansky became more obvious. Why were the automatic sprinklers not working? They would have drastically reduced the extent of the damage and the death-toll. The answer was very simple. There were no automatic sprinklers; Barney Welansky had not considered it necessary to waste money on such trivialities.

A strangely macabre sight greeted the first fireman to batter his way through into the Melody Lounge. There were people still sitting at the bar, apparently unconcerned. Some still had drinks in their hands. But they were all motionless. It was as if he had wandered into some ghastly wax tableau.

Then he realized the horrifying truth. These people were all frozen in death. They had been asphyxiated by the fumes and the smoke.

The intensive search of the Cocoanut Grove also produced more facts which Barney Welansky had managed to keep secret. More than 4000 cases of wines and liquor were found hidden away on the premises. They were tucked behind the false walls of the Melody Lounge, slotted into the ceilings over the men's and ladies' lounges.

The reason for them being kept hidden was soon apparent. Welansky had obtained them illicitly without paying any tax on them. That was in line with the way he ran his business: squeezing out as much profit as possible while running it as cheaply as possible. He did not even carry any public-liability insurance to cover his clients against injury or death. That sort of policy involved outlaying money. But now the consequences of this cheapskate behavior were brought home to him.

The Cocoanut Grove was declared bankrupt. Creditors waived their priority claims on the assets so that these could be distributed amongst the survivors and the relatives of the dead who had filed claims.

Awkward questions also started being asked about the role the authorities had played in ensuring the safety of clients at the Cocoanut Grove.

Boston theaters at that time were required to spray fire-proofing chemicals over inflammable decorations. Places like the Cocoanut Grove were not required to comply with this regulation. However, precautionary checks had been made. An official of the Boston Fire Prevention Division said that he had

Of those who escaped death on that fearful night, 181 were wounded —perhaps crippled or disfigured for life by the fire. Among the guests was the celebrated singing cowboy, Buck Jones. He had gone to the Cocoanut Grove to relax after a strenuous day selling war bonds—and died there.

inspected the club only eight days before the fire and had found no cause for concern. He claimed that he had tested the decorations by holding a lighted match to them. This did not explain why they had flared so horrifically when the waiter had accidentally touched them with his match.

And why had the police not taken action over the blatant over-crowding? Allegations of laxity and negligence in high places were thrown around. But, after many public and private arguments, the bulk of the blame was placed on Barney Welansky.

He was found guilty of manslaughter and was sentenced to serve from 12 to 15 years. However, he was released after being in prison for three years and seven months because he was suffering from terminal cancer. Four months after his release, he died.

Dramatic changes were made in the code to protect the public—in Boston and in other places around the world—as a direct result of the disaster. That, however, was little consolation to those who were maimed or bereaved. For them, nothing could ever erase the horror of the night the Cocoanut Grove turned into an incendiary bomb.

Grab your top hat ... we're off to outer space!

The mighty thrust of a spacebound rocket is an everyday sight ... but in the 19th century the first science-fiction artists were more concerned with how you dressed to meet the Martians.

Anthony Frewin

Anthony Frewin

An interplanetary space rocket lies where it has just landed, on the desolate surface of the Moon. Three astronauts have clambered out; the attitudes of each one reflecting awe and wonderment at their strange surroundings.

And there the resemblance to what *we* now know about lunar landings ends. For already one of the men—dressed in a natty three-piece suit with watch-and-chain—is puffing contentedly at a cigarette. Another sits scribbling, presumably committing to paper his poetic description of the scene, while the third takes 'lunar measurements' on what looks suspiciously like a highway architect's theodolite.

This is the thrill of interplanetary exploration, seen in strictly 19th-century terms by the artist who, in 1865, illustrated Jules Verne's forward-looking science-fiction novel, *From the Earth to the Moon.*

Clearly, the 'writer' in the picture is composing something more resounding than 'a small step for man, a giant leap for mankind', but why is he not wearing an oxygen mask? To that absurd question the artist Hildebrand would no doubt have made the unanswerable reply, "Because, sir, he would have to remove his top hat!"

Flights of Fancy

The depiction of space probes, rocket ships and the astronauts who guide them has fired artists to extraordinary 'flights of fancy' since the days of Jules Verne.

It was a long time, however, before they could break free of existing 'images'. Early spacecraft looked like

1865: in the 100 years between the publishing of Jules Verne's *From the Earth to the Moon* (left) and the Apollo landing, man had much to learn about lunar atmosphere.
1887: (above) "We perceived the cars of the Mercurians floating in space," taking the air—presumably—like their Earthly counterparts.

seagoing vessels with wings. Then it was the turn of a hybrid 'aerial submarine'. As airships were invented, fictional spacecraft hurriedly adopted the familiar cigar-shape, eventually sprouting hundreds of propellers as aircraft technology advanced.

Jet Set

In the 1930s, all space-flight problems were solved by 'artistic creations' which were recognizably airplanes despite the bulbous and exaggerated aerodynamics. The invention of jet propulsion was a further boon to illustrators and artists, who played every variation on the rocket form until their minds finally exploded into today's super-scientific marvels of SF wizardry.

No such problems worried one Paul Hardy, who provided the artwork for a SF story in the *English Illustrated Magazine* in 1887. The tale described a British Empire-building expedition to Mercury, presumably destined to be the first of Her Majesty Queen Victoria's cosmic colonies.

Hardy's rather vague spacecraft looks as though it would have been more at home under the Atlantic. Disdaining protective clothing or oxygen supplies, the cosmonauts stand on the conning-tower watching 'the cars of the Mercu-

rians floating towards us'. It was that sort of stiff upper-lip behavior which had always impressed other natives on Earth, so why shouldn't it work in outer space?

Barely 50 years later, things had changed radically in the rocket-illustration world. No stiff upper-lip tradition supports the hapless cosmonauts whose sharklike craft has crashed on the deserts of Mars. Something very nasty happened before they managed to totter as far as the cover of February 1939's *Astounding Science Fiction,* judging by the pathetic little cross below the flight-ladder. Despite the relatively convincing spacecraft, present-day readers can immediately grasp the reason for the cosmonaut's discomfort —oxygen masks had apparently still not caught on in polite SF circles.

Unfriendly Natives

The biggest single difference between the way 19th-century artists visualized space flights and later developments concerns the dangers involved. Before World War One, Earthly astronauts tended to bring all the benefits of an advanced civilization to barbarous and benighted Mercurians, Venusians, Martians and Moonmen. Later, it was *we* who were confronted with all the evidence of a superior technology . . . and often got badly mauled and thoroughly shamed in the encounter.

In *Amazing Stories* of August 1930, the cover artist ingeniously shows the 'innards' of his caterpillar-like spacecraft. The turbines and generators (compulsory in all 1930s illustrations) are neatly exposed when the craft is decapitated by an alien space module (yet more

turbines and generators) looking like a ghostly goldfish bowl.

Howard Brown took a more optimistic view of space travel in his *Startling Stories* cover of November 1939. Just to prove that no idea is too well-known to be used again, he visualized a spaceship about to take off—with a considerable cargo of livestock—on a Noah's Ark journey to another planet.

Although his craft bears more than a passing resemblance to a fairground roller-coaster, the idea was oddly prophetic. Scientists today are toying with the idea of preserving endangered species in a 'space zoo' which could form part of a satellite city suspended between Earth and the Moon.

The same city-in-the-sky idea was used vividly by Arthur C. Clarke in *2001* and superbly realized by artist Bruce Pennington on the first-edition cover of Britain's *Science Fiction Monthly* in 1974, when we were already well into the Space Age.

The depiction of spacecraft and other 'cosmic runabouts' is now firmly backed by sound scientific knowledge. Unlike the early illustrators, who desperately avoided technological details, modern illustrators can—and irrepressibly do—revel in them.

'Fictoid' Facts?

In the realm of space travel, at least, science fact has almost overtaken science fiction. American author Norman Mailer once coined the word 'factoid' for something fictional which had come to be accepted as fact. Maybe SF needs a proud new word to cover all those imaginative designs which, decades later, became reality. How about 'fictoid'?

1930: *Amazing Stories* blinds its eager subscribers with contemporary science.
1939: the possibility of space disaster rears its ugly head.
1939: 'get away from it all' by courtesy of *Startling Stories.*
1974: fact or fiction? The confidence of early sci-fi believers is ultimately rewarded.

One area of SF art, however, has never left the wild world of fantasy. In the representation of Creatures from Outer Space, some of the nightmare forms dreamed up by illustrators had to be seen to be disbelieved . . .

MY LIFE OF BOOZE, BROADS AND BEDLAM

Keystone

For Manville the Marrying Millionaire, life was one long peal of wedding bells . . . interrupted by scenes, fights, alimony and the constant flash of photographers' bulbs. He married 11 times but never once found complete domestic bliss. The wives were still feuding at his funeral.

The 'battle of the blondes' started on the afternoon that ex-showgirl Marcelle Edwards—the fourth wife of multi-millionaire Tommy Manville—came home to find that her husband had locked *her* out of their Long Island mansion, and had locked *himself* inside it with his new blonde secretary. Used to such happenings, the long-legged Marcelle thought nothing of scaling the 11-foot chain-link fencing around Bon Repos, and of avoiding the special guards he had employed to keep her out. However, when she discovered the secretary, Dolly Goering, barring the front door, Marcelle literally went for her tooth and nail.

"Whaddya mean, there's no room for me!" she screamed at Dolly. "There's more than twenty bedrooms in this goddamned place! Get the hell out of it and let me in!"

But Dolly had her orders. She refused to budge and so Marcelle reacted like the 'vicious bitch' her husband said she was. She slugged Dolly on the jaw, put a wrestler's grip on her, and then grabbed her by the hair and dragged her by its dark roots into the house. There she vainly looked around for Thomas F. Manville Junior, who was hiding in a closet, with the door partly open so that he could see the 'fun'.

As Marcelle glowered around the hall, Dolly made a recovery and fought back, seizing her adversary by the throat. For the next few minutes the blondes punched, scratched and screamed their way around the area. Their clothes were ripped and almost torn off and it was clear that one, or both of them, could be badly hurt.

It was then that Tommy Manville showed his grinning face. But, instead of trying to restrain the incensed women and restore the peace, he rushed up onto the roof of Bon Repos—which stood in $3\frac{1}{2}$ luscious acres at Premium Point—and began sounding the siren installed there.

Minutes later, the house was alive with police and newspapermen, who dashed inside beneath the sign stating unequivocally: 'Beware. Marrying Manville Lives Here'. The result of what Manville joyfully called the 'bitch-fight' was a caution to keep his household in calmer order in future, and the privilege of making the front page of nearly every New York paper the next morning.

It was the summer of 1937 and the Milwaukee-born Tommy Manville was 43 years old. He had $13 million securely invested ('Lucky thirteen', he called it); he existed on the interest of more than $1 million a year; and he had 30 years of riotous living and another seven glamorous if pugnacious wives ahead of him.

Manville blamed his 'addiction to

All pictures A.P.

women'—especially busty, come-up-and-see-me-sometime blondes—on his father and grandfather, the founders of the family asbestos fortune. They had both been notorious womanizers and Manville resented the fact that his parents divorced in 1908, when he was aged 14.

His sympathies were for his mother, whom he lovingly called 'Duchess', and he despised the way his father 'made a middle-aged fool of himself' with a wiggle of chorus-girls and no-hope actresses. However, the Duchess was just as foolish as her ex-husband when it came to money and she was constantly in debt and being pursued by bailiffs.

"It got so we daren't answer any knock

at the door of our New York apartment," Manville complained later. "But at least I learnt one thing from my mother—how to be good and mean. I've never in my life had any genuine money troubles. I just pretended to be broke to cut down on my alimony payments.

"From my father I guess I inherited nothing but his weakness for women. With his example I should have stayed a bachelor for life. But I had his blood, his urges in me, and I could resist anything but the temptation of another honeymoon!"

Marrying Manville left his expensive boarding school at the age of 16 and found himself suited and fit for nothing.

Keystone

A.P.

A.P.

A.P.

His father kept him short of money and he was forced to take a succession of manual jobs. "It got so I had so many blisters on my hands," he said, "that I couldn't have held a silver dollar even if I'd had one. There was only one thing to do about it—I decided to get married!"

For *the first Mrs Manville* he chose the fair-haired Florence Huber, whom he met in June 1911 in the lobby of New York's New Amsterdam theater. She was aged 23 (six years older than the love-smitten Tommy) and was as small as she was dogged. According to Manville, she was a former Ziegfeld girl ("She must have been one of Ziggie's few midgets," cracked a friend), and they

arranged to become man and wife after knowing each other for only four days.

Sensing that his son-and-heir was being given the 'cupid's rush', Mr Manville Senior sent detectives to New York City Hall to declare the bridegroom under age—"and out of his mind," added the tycoon privately. However, the teenager was as determined as he was foolish. He and Miss Huber eloped to Jersey City and were married there.

"I'll love Tommy for always," the bride declared. But her husband's affections were shorter lived. He began to fight with the gray-eyed blonde who declared herself to be 'just a simple country girl from Pennsylvania'. (Later, when she

Some of the women who—by the time he had got to wife No. 8 (center)—had won Tommy the title of 'Marrying Manville'. From the top (left): No. 1, Florence Huber; No. 2, Lois McCoin; No. 3, Avonne Taylor; No. 4 (above left), Marcelle Edwards; No. 6 (above) Billie Boze. The odd woman out is secretary Dolly Goering (above right). He didn't marry her.

went to law for a share of the Manville millions, it was disclosed that, before snaring Tommy, she had been a prostitute, sharing her earnings and her apartment on New York's 42nd Street with a colored boyfriend.)

33

Tommy's health suffered, he became depressed and irritable, and then went down with acute appendicitis. Needing money for an operation, he telephoned his father asking for a loan. "You're on your own now, son," Manville senior replied. "You can have your fun without me and you can suffer without me, too."

The operation was therefore performed—and badly—in a New York charity hospital. Tommy never fully recovered from it and was in sporadic pain until 1954, when he finally had corrective surgery performed. "I guess I suffered all that agony for so long just to remind myself what an old bastard my father was," explained Manville.

With his marriage on the rocks ("You could say it was never off them," he remarked), and with the United States entering World War One, in April 1917 Manville got work chauffeuring naval VIPs to and from their bases. It wasn't until 1922, the fourth year of peace, that he at last divorced Florence and acquired some emotional peace himself.

"No Good on My Own"

At first he enjoyed his freedom from the prolonged and bitter court battles with Florence. But he soon became bored, lonely, and filled with self-pity. "I'm no good on my own," he declared. "I've just got to have a little wifey—even if it's one whom I come to hate and quarrel with. Anything's better than no wife and no scraps!"

So, in August 1925 he swiftly courted and promptly proposed to Lois McCoin, a young honey-blonde secretary in his father's New York office. Once again, Manville Senior disapproved and renewed his threat to disinherit his son. But Tommy didn't give a piece of confetti for his father's displeasure. "I'll marry Lois," he stated, "and if Dad still refuses us his blessing, then I'll take a wife in each State of the Union—marrying one as fast as I can get the previous nuptials dissolved!"

The wedding took place, Lois became *the second Mrs Manville,* and a short while later old Mr Manville died of a heart attack. At the age of 31 Tommy finally came into his inheritance (he and his sister Lorraine split the $26 million down the middle), and was free to marry—and divorce—as he pleased.

His first marriage had lasted 11 years, and his second fought its way through to five. After the arguments, partings, reconciliations, police actions and court appearances that were becoming his marital trademark, Manville and Lois were divorced in 1930. They had actually lived together for only a few months, but it seemed, said Manville, "like a long season in hell, with the Devil being a woman for once."

However, preferring to have company

in Hell than be on his own in Heaven, Manville remarried a few days after the divorce came through. *The third Mrs Manville* was yet another 'dark blonde', Avonne Taylor, who really had been in the Ziegfeld Follies and whom the great producer had labelled, "The most beautiful woman ever to appear on the American stage."

But it took more than beauty to stay married to Manville. It took what no mere woman seemed to have. For, 28 days after the wedding ceremony, Manville and Avonne parted for ever. "I knew when I agreed to marry him," she stated, "that it wouldn't last. I even got a $100 000 cheque in settlement for a divorce at the wedding reception! He was kind of thoughtful that way."

By this time (with Lois being awarded alimony of $19 000 a year for life) Man-

ville was becoming noted as a kind of financial Jekyll and Hyde. A frequenter of New York's nightclubs, musical shows, and speakeasies, he described his life as 'Booze, Broads and Bedlam!' However, he was as mean as he was amorous and one head waiter accused him of sneaking in his own bread-rolls and biscuits so that he wouldn't have to pay for any food.

He rarely, if ever, left a tip, and at least once was seen to take a $5 bill meant for a waiter and slip it into his pocket. His one main extravagance was his Long Island house, Bon Repos, with its 40 rooms, private theater, and mammoth garage in which he kept his fleet of Rolls Royces.

He developed a love of policemen, journalists, photographers, and gangsters. He scrambled to be in their com-

Wife No. 7, Sunny Ainsworth (top left), lasted only one night; No. 8, Georgina Campbell (far left), endured 5 weeks before there was a separation. No. 9, the pugnacious Anita Roddy-Eden, who claimed to have been illegally divorced by Tommy, almost came near to bankrupting him. When she brought an action for increased maintenance, he claimed in court to be down to his last $2 million.

pany and flushed with pride whenever someone like the racketeer Jack 'Legs' Diamond flipped a hand at him in a Broadway restaurant. He became obsessed with guns and always carried one with him, "Just in case some jealous so-and-so tries any funny stuff," he explained.

Indeed, as any one of his past or future wives could testify, he was something of an expert in jealousy. If he saw one of his spouses talking to another man she was accused of infidelity and perversion. If she had lunch with a girlfriend then he branded her a 'lesbian'. Waiters, cab-drivers, stewards, hairdressers (of either sex), maids, secretaries, chauffeurs and delivery-boys were all accused at one time or another of having slept with one, if not all, of his 11 wives.

"He was," said a manfriend, "one of the most insecure people you could hope not to meet. To Tommy, every woman in sight was after his fortune. Then, when he married one of them, every man and woman in sight was after his bride. It was pathetic, really, because he could be as nice and kind and generous as anyone. Then he got to thinking about his father—and then he was a beast!"

This was the situation when, in October 1933, Marcelle Edwards became *the fourth Mrs Manville.* The marriage lasted—if that was the word—for four years of non-stop bickering and fights. The tussle with Dolly Goering (who moved into the mansion and the Manvilles' lives after answering an advertisement stating, 'Tommy Manville needs a secretary. If you're blonde, apply at Bon Repos, Premium Point'), marked the end of their co-habitation.

"Tommy had many good points," said Marcelle on taking the first plane to Reno. "The problem was in knowing whether he would greet me with tears of joy or tears of rage. And whichever one it was, you didn't always know the reason or cause of it—if you'd done something to please him or otherwise. It was like living with an unruly child that would gush with delight one minute and rant with rage the next!"

To celebrate his divorce from Marcelle, Manville decided to make his first (and, as it turned out, last) trip abroad. With a chorus-line of blondes he decided to visit England for the coronation, in May 1937, of King George VI. "I guess me and my girls will brighten up that old Westminster Abbey," he told newsmen before planning to sail from New York. "We might just have ourselves a ball over there."

However, the ball never took place. On learning of Manville's intentions, the British Government announced that he and his champagne-haired companions would not be allowed to land at Southampton. No official reason was given for the ban, but it was obvious that no marriage could fully be regarded as sacred and lasting if Tommy was around.

Bon Repos

Saddened, but not deterred, by this implied criticism of his life-style, Manville looked around for another bride to come to blows with him in the farcically-named Bon Repos, or Good Rest. For *the fifth Mrs Manville,* he chose dancer Bonita 'Bonnie' Edwards, whom he married in November 1941. Seventeen days later she hit the trail for Reno and Tommy saw her off at the station. Wearing a black arm-band, and with the customary photographer in attendance, he mournfully sang 'Bring Back My Bonnie To Me' and waved until the train was out of sight.

Exactly a year later (distressed because the news of World War Two in Europe was crowding him off the front pages), he found a blonde who was prepared to become *the sixth Mrs Manville.* He proposed to young Billie Boze 15 minutes after they met, was accepted on the spot, and was divorced from her 60 days later—with the marriage unconsummated.

It was now no secret that Manville preferred headline glory to girls, and that he would do anything and marry almost anyone to get his name into print. Once, when things were strangely quiet on the marital front, he rode a horse into Leon and Eddie's nightclub on New York's 52nd Street. Then he planted a wartime 'Victory Garden' at Bon Repos, and was photographed holding a blonde in shorts in one arm and a rake in the other.

Another nine months went by (months in which there were more blondes, more parties, more bust-ups, more publicity), and then *the seventh Mrs Manville* —career girl Macie 'Sunny' Ainsworth —put her name to a marriage certificate. Six hours later, on returning to their suite at the Savoy Plaza Hotel, New York, they parted after Manville received what he called a 'sinister telephone call'.

A Mockery

According to him, the caller said in tough, gangster tones, "Forget about this marriage, Romeo, or the boys in Chicago will be buying you a new suit—a cement one!" This time he didn't bother about an arm-band or a lament. He despatched Sunny to Reno, where she collected $17 000 compensation for her trouble, and where the *Reno Journal* ran an editorial complaining that Marrying Manville was making a 'mockery' of their courts.

It took Manville two years to recover from the experience. Then, shortly before Christmas 1945, he was interviewed by a British reporter, Georgina Campbell, who found the most significant question directed at her. "Will you marry me?" demanded Manville. She said yes, became *the eighth Mrs Manville*, and five weeks later hit him over the head with a frying-pan and so brought about their legal separation.

But it was death, not divorce, that ended their union permanently. After falling from a horse and seriously injuring herself in 1948, Georgina recovered after Manville had generously paid for her hospital treatment and plastic surgery. Then, early on the morning of April 26, 1952, she was driving to Bon Repos to have breakfast with him when she was involved in an accident and killed.

Shocked by the tragedy, Manville waited a decent period before selecting *the ninth Mrs Manville*—the blonde and spirited Anita Frances Roddy-Eden, who became his biographer and who claims that she is still married to him! Their wedding took place in July 1952, and after the usual upsets (during which he shot her in the foot and, on another occasion, broke down her bedroom door with an axe) he decided she must take a fast plane to Reno.

However, Anita (a writer, dancer and musician) refused to legally break their bonds. So, sly as a satyr, Manville sent her twin sister, Juanita, to Reno to pose as Anita during a divorce action. The trick worked and Manville was free to seek *the tenth Mrs Manville*—tall, blonde Patricia Gaston, who was not, as it turned out, to enjoy the spats and splendors of life at Bon Repos.

For some time past Manville claimed

he had been haunted by the ghost of *the eighth Mrs Manville*, whose psychic manifestations drove him to sell his mansion and move into a modest, red-brick cottage in Chappaqua. But former showgirl Patricia hated the quiet life, and she particularly objected to Manville's 'brutal' treatment of her. Less than four months later she, too, had added to the 'mockery' of the Reno divorce courts and so *the eleventh Mrs Manville* bravely took her place.

Manville's health was already failing when he married a black-haired German, the attractive Christina Erdlen. She was to be the last Mrs Manville and she and her sister, Frieda, nursed and closely guarded the millionaire during his final years of illness . . . the result of decades of heavy drinking.

He lived as a recluse, with Christina censoring all telephone calls and dis-

couraging all visitors. Not even his personal doctor saw much of him, and was forced to prescribe drugs and medicine by phone. He was too weak and tired to fight any more with anyone, and put up no struggle when he died on October 8, 1967 at the age of 73.

Funeral Wrangle

He had lived without dignity and went out in the same way. Both *the ninth Mrs Manville* (Anita Roddy-Eden, who had been unable to expose the Reno deception for fear that her twin sister would go to jail) and *the eleventh Mrs Manville* claimed to be his legal widow. This ensured that his estate would be legally tied-up for years, with no one benefiting from it. At the same time *the first Mrs Manville* (Florence Huber, then aged 80) surfaced and demanded an autopsy on the body of the man she declared she had 'loved for the past 56 years'.

Her request was refused, and at the funeral itself Manville created his last headlines before being put to rest. *The ninth Mrs Manville* placed a red rose on

Patricia Gaston—No. 10 (top)—complained of brutal treatment at the hands of 58-year-old Tommy; No. 11, Christina Erdlen, survived his death. He had managed to spend over $1 250 000 in marriage settlements.

his coffin in New York's Episcopal Church on Fifth Avenue—only to have it dashed to the ground by *the eleventh Mrs Manville*.

In her book about Marrying Manville, *The Lives and Wives of Tommy Manville*, Anita wonders if her late husband is "still having a great time chasing blonde angels? . . . One thing is certain . . . he won't be alone but will surely have a blonde on his arm. Knowing my husband as I do, I'm sure he won't be faithful but will have an eye out for 'a new girl in town'."

Marrying Manville's life may have been one long wedding procession, but, despite the succession of spouses, he died childless. "I loathe kids and I don't want any of my own," he once said.

JUST A MATTER OF TIME

No greater obstacle stands in the way of space travel than time. It is the key to the problem of vast distances. Yet time itself is an enigma. Will we ever be able to travel through the time barrier, shrinking the centuries, becoming almost ageless as light-years flash past? Or is there an unknown hazard which would isolate an astronaut in a 'world without end'?

Illustration by Mick Brownfield

'I suppose a suicide who holds a pistol to his skull feels much the same wonder at what will come next as I felt then. I took the starting lever in one hand and the stopping one in the other, pressed the first and almost immediately the second. I seemed to reel; I felt a nightmare sensation of falling; and, looking round, I saw the laboratory as before . . . Then I noted the clock. A moment before, as it seemed, it had stood at a minute or so past ten. Now it was nearly half past three!'

In those gripping words, novelist H. G. Wells began a 'journey' which has fascinated scientists ever since. In his book *The Time Machine*, he visualized man traveling at ease through the fourth dimension; through Time itself.

Since then, many of Wells's equally fantastic predictions have become fact. Yet time travel still remains as impossible as landing on the Moon must have seemed in Wells's time.

Despite all the obstacles, is it possible that we *will* learn to travel in time, as we have been able to reach the Moon?

The greatest obstacle of all is the nature of time itself. It is an enigma. Even defining it is a problem. For it has a different nature from that of space.

Whereas space envelops us and we can move about in it at will, time is more like a conveyor belt on which we are trapped, moving inexorably forward. We have not yet learned to reverse the direction of the conveyor belt . . . or even whether that is possible.

Normally, we take time for granted as something shown on a clock. But a clock is only a way of measuring the flow of time, and tells us nothing about what we are measuring. Turning back the clock does not reverse the flow of time.

Our familiar daily time scales are based on the rotation of the Earth, yet even here there are problems and paradoxes. All long-distance travelers are used to making little trips backwards or forwards in time as they move from one time zone to another. Indeed, the first men to circumnavigate the globe, survivors of Magellan's crew, were puzzled to arrive back in Spain in 1522 a day later than they calculated. (In *Around the World in 80 Days*, Phileas Fogg arrived back a day sooner, because he circumnavigated the globe in the opposite direction to Magellan's crew.) Nowadays we prevent this by dropping or adding a day when crossing the International Date Line, on the opposite side of the globe to the Greenwich meridian.

When originally set up, the date line ran exactly along the 180° meridian, cutting through an island in the Fiji group with the result that separate villages on the island lived a day apart. Unscrupulous estate owners moved their slaves from side to side of the date line so that they never had a Sunday. Shops whose premises straddled the 180° line built two entrances, one in each hemisphere (and in different days) so that they could legally avoid the Sunday closing that missionaries tried to enforce.

The Time Game

By moving across the date line, newspaper readers could read the *Fiji Times* the day before it came out—or even before some of the news had happened. These anomalies were removed when the date line was moved out to sea. It now bends around all land areas, placing them firmly in one day or the next.

These small-scale time slippages are just a result of the way we measure time, rather than a reversal of the flow of time itself. The inexorable march of events into what we term The Future was called by the British physicist Sir

Illustration by Mick Brownfield

Speech bubbles in image: "EEP SPACE — E UNKNOWN!", "AS THE SHIP ACCELERATES TOWARDS THE SPEED OF LIGHT....", "ITS CLOCKS SLOW ALMOST TO A STANDSTILL...", "ANDING — BUT AS DON 'ES TO GREET THE CROWD...!", "HI DAD!", "WELCOME HOME DARLING!", "GOOD LORD! 'CHOKE:.... MARGE? TIMMY?", "ENDS"

Arthur Eddington 'the arrow of time'. Can we reverse time's arrow—or is there a deep physical law that prevents us?

Most of the events we see happen only one way: for instance, the flowing of radiation from a star. We regard such an event as irreversible in time. The American physicist Richard Feynman has described the apparent irreversibility of events in everyday life by reference to scrambled eggs: the scrambling of eggs denotes the direction of time's arrow.

In practice, of course, eggs don't become unscrambled—yet there is nothing absurd *in theory* about the reversal of such an event. If we chose to do so, all the atoms of the egg could be unscrambled to make a new, fresh egg, like running a film backwards.

There are many events we can easily imagine in reverse: for instance, the lobbing of a tennis ball over a net, which in the real world works equally well in both directions. This is indeed a time-reversible event. The rotation of the Earth on its axis, and its motion in orbit around the Sun, are time-reversible events. When we calculate the dates of ancient eclipses we mathematically run the Earth and Moon backwards in time, like when a planetarium projector is reversed to show ancient skies.

So is there an absolute direction to the arrow of time, something more fundamental than the scrambling of eggs? Until recently, scientists have thought not. They have accepted that there is a basic symmetry to the Universe which fails to distinguish any absolutes.

But there is now a hint that, on the atomic scale, not all reactions are time reversible: there may be an absolute reference for time's arrow in certain rare interactions involving an obscure atomic particle known as the neutral K meson. If so, the laws of nature might really be different in some cases if time flowed backwards. But no one has any real idea how significant the differences are, and in any case evidence for this apparent time asymmetry is not conclusive.

Since the 1930s, scientists have thought about anti-Universes, in which everything is a reversal of what we know in ours. They predicted that each atomic particle would have its own anti-particle, and the symmetry of the Universe has indeed been proved in this case by the discovery of anti-particles. The first of these, the *positron*, was found in 1932. It is an electron with a positive charge. Since then, Richard Feynman has shown that the positron can be considered as an electron moving backwards in time, and this concept of time-reversal has been extended to describe the behavior of all anti-particles. However, this development is of limited value to would-be time travelers because a clock made of anti-particles would still tick forwards, not backwards.

More interestingly for would-be time travelers, some scientists have imagined the existence of a total mirror-image Universe in which time's arrow would point backwards relative to us. Judged by our time direction, light would flow into stars, and we would therefore find such a Universe to be invisible! Even if we could get a message across, it would be immediately forgotten because it would become part of the anti-Universe's future.

British physicist F. Russell Stannard once drew the picture of two parallel Universes in which time unfolded in different directions. Each Universe would be unaware of the other. But if, in imagination, they could view each other, each would see events in the other's Universe happening backwards. Yet, to the observer, everything would happen normally in his own Universe.

Theorists have taken UFOs to be possible travelers from other Universes. On a much more scientific level, some astronomers have suggested that the mysterious space phenomena known as Black Holes—stars more than 2½ times bigger than our Sun undergoing a collapse so powerful that no known forces can stop it—could be 'short cuts' into another dimension. "Were we to plunge down a Black Hole, we would emerge, it is conjectured, in a different part of the Universe and in another epoch in time," writes Dr Carl Sagan in *The Cosmic Connection*. "For all we do know, Black Holes are the transportation conduits of advanced technological civilizations; conceivably conduits in time as well as space."

Taking the theory one logical stage further, Black Holes should open out into a Universe parallel to ours. On the receiving end, all the matter pouring out of *our* Universe down the drain plug of a Black Hole should appear as a white hole in the parallel Universe.

Astrophysicist Robert Hjellming has proposed that quasar stars or even the centers of galaxies could be the white holes where material pours into our ken from the Black Holes of a parallel Universe. Black Holes, and other theoretical chinks in the fabric of space called wormholes proposed by the American physicist John A. Wheeler of Princeton, could provide time-tunnels to elsewhere—and elsewhen.

Sir Arthur Eddington believed that the direction of time's arrow was governed by the expanding Universe. Therefore, there could be only one direction for time. From this has come the concept that, if the Universe oscillates alternately outwards and inwards as some astronomers have suggested, then the collapsing phase could lead to a reversal of the arrow of time.

This is an unsatisfactory idea, because of the strange limbo there would be as the Universe slowed its outward expansion and finally began to fall in again. How would the arrow of time 'know' when to reverse? A successful new theory was published in 1972 by Paul Davies of King's College, London. Dr Davies proposes that in each subsequent cycle of the oscillating Universe the arrow of time is reversed. The Universe, therefore, has two different states which are repeated endlessly, like the continual flipping of a coin. After two expansions and contractions, the heads-and-tails Universe is back to where it started. That means that *this* cycle will be repeated after the next oscillation—and our future is thus like a pre-recorded film awaiting a screening. . . .

One Way Only

However, the latest evidence from astronomers shows that the Universe does not oscillate, but that its expansion will continue forever—the arrow of time continue to point in one direction only.

A little-known loophole of significance for time-travelers has been provided by the Czech-born American mathematician Kurt Gödel, who found some solutions to Einstein's equations of general relativity which indicated that one could, in certain circumstances, go back in time and meet oneself. No one has been able to prove that such a circumstance would exist in the real Universe, and Gödel's work remains a mathematical curiosity that has been largely ignored by other scientists because of the contradictions that arise with travel into the past—for instance, returning to shoot your father before you are born. In science, such paradoxes or logical impasses signify an impossibility.

In search of a deep-lying explanation for the apparently immutable forward flow of time, many scientists have adopted the view that the flow of time is marked by the loss of information in a system. As in the case of the scrambled eggs or the flow of radiation from a star, there is a decrease in the orderliness of matter with time. This is linked with the suggestion that the Universe is 'running down'—that there will come a time when all the energy in the Universe is distributed uniformly as heat.

Recently, however, astronomy professor David Layzer of Harvard University has equated the direction of time's arrow with an *increase* in the amount of infor-

mation in the Universe. For instance, the growing of a plant, the aging of a star, and the changing face of the Earth and Moon all show an increase of information with advancing time. One might say that the arrow of time is like a train in which all seats face away from the engine; we learn about where we've come from, not about where we're going.

Professor Layzer has traced the underlying cause of this back to the state of the Universe shortly after its origin in a 'big bang' explosion, from which it has been expanding ever since. The matter of the Universe was initially in a smooth, structureless state, from which it broke up into fragments as it expanded, forming increasingly complex systems of stars, galaxies, and clusters of galaxies. "The intuitive perception of the world as unfolding in time captures one of the most deep-seated properties of the Universe," he concludes.

This clearly indicates that, although we can use machinery to reverse normal physical processes, such as when we use a refrigerator to keep an object cooler than its surroundings, a universal clock was irreversibly set running at the big bang. Like the pull of gravity, the forward flow of time seems to be one of the fundamental properties of the Universe it is impossible to switch off.

Ticket To Nowhere

Such a conclusion confirms Eddington's long-standing opinion about a one-way time system, and appears to answer the question of time travel in the negative. Since the past is, so to speak, already accounted for, that is perhaps not surprising. Yet, while going against the flow of time seems forbidden by the traffic laws of the Universe, traveling *with* the arrow of time into the future is another matter. It is not always realized that the laws of physics firmly embody the principle of time-travel into the future—albeit on a one-way ticket.

Although time is everywhere forward-moving, the *rate* at which it advances varies for different observers. The fact that there is no absolute time, only relative time, was first perceived by Albert Einstein in his special theory of relativity, published in 1905. The theory of special relativity has been amply confirmed by scientists, even to the extent of flying an accurate atomic clock around the globe; when compared with an identical counterpart that had remained stationary in Washington, the jet-setting clock was found to differ by a few billionths of a second, as theory predicted. This time-difference effect is known as *time dilation*.

The amount of time difference depends on the relative speeds of objects. Everyday speeds are so slow that the effect of time dilation is negligible. But

in a super-high-speed spaceship its effect mounts up dramatically.

Time dilation is a natural consequence of the fact that the speed of light is the speed limit of the Universe. No matter how hard we accelerate, or for how long, we can never quite reach the speed of light. But as a space traveler inches closer to this limiting speed, so his clock will slow almost to a standstill relative to its regularly ticking counterpart on Earth. The effect is not confined to clocks alone—everything on board the ship, including the biological processes of aging, would be slowed by the same amount. Therefore a traveler aboard the spacecraft would notice nothing amiss —until he returned to Earth to find his sons older than himself. . . .

Like moving between time zones on Earth, therefore, traveling in time also means traveling in space. But to the adventurous, that is a bonus—because time dilation puts the Universe within our grasp. A man could travel to other galaxies inside a human lifetime.

Lonely Traveler

Here are the results of calculations by the American astronomer Carl Sagan of Cornell University. Let us assume that we board an imaginary starship of the future capable of traveling with an acceleration of one gravity—that is, the same force as exerted on us by the Earth's gravity. Under these conditions, everything on board the ship would feel the same as on Earth. After about one year of Earth time at such acceleration, the ship would be traveling close to the speed of light. The astronauts would have aged only a few years by the time they reached the nearest stars; they will have counted off a mere 21 years by the time they reached the center of our Galaxy, 30 000 light years away.

Of course, we must realize that this form of time travel may be strictly one-way. Some scientists contend that distance may be subject to the same shrinking effects of relativity as time—reducing a space-journey to more manageable proportions—but most believe that an astronaut who set out to travel among the galaxies in his near-the-speed-of-light starship might never have a home to return to, for the Earth and its Sun may both have died by the time his wandering is over.

In our search for the key to time travel, would this, then, be the sacrifice man would have to make? In overcoming the greatest of all scientific obstacles, could our space explorer of the future become an inter-galactic Flying Dutchman, doomed for ever to wander the stars as Earth aged and shrivelled behind him? It is the kind of awesome prospect which would even have halted the pen of H. G. Wells.

THE TERROR THAT HOWLS

The court was stunned. "Yes," admitted the prisoner, "I am a werewolf." Once more, a legend that had haunted men since the beginning of time emerged in all too tangible form to rend, kill and devour.

From the darkest depths of superstition, a terror had emerged to spread fear throughout the whole of Gascony, in the south-west of France. Young children had mysteriously begun to disappear from hamlets and villages, particularly in the St Sever area. At first, the peasants blamed wolves, but as the attacks continued, older people crossed themselves and whispered of something worse. From mouth to mouth spread the single, dreaded word, 'Werewolf!'

Few words possess more powerful overtones of fear. The idea of a witch or wizard who can change from human to animal shape to kill and rend strikes deep at the subconscious. In 1945, the German dictator, Adolf Hitler, was able to inspire his last-ditch 'People's Army' by urging them to "harass the enemy like werewolves."

But in the St Sever area in 1603 there was no 'enemy', merely innocent children plucked from their homes and hideously savaged. The panic had reached the stage of mass hysteria when three witnesses went to one of the local magistrates. They told an extraordinary story. One of them, 13-year-old Marguerite Poirier, swore that during a full moon she had been attacked by a savage beast "much resembling a wolf." She had been tending her cattle at the time and only managed to save herself from being severely bitten by flailing at the beast with her stout, iron-pointed staff.

But it was the testimony of the second witness, 18-year-old Jeanne Gaboriaut, which shook the magistrate. The girl described how she, too, had been looking after her cattle when she had been approached by a 14-year-old youth named Jean Grenier who, like her, was a servant of a wealthy farmer, Pierre Combaut, of the parish of Esperons. Grenier started to make advances and boasted that he would marry her, despite her reluctance. When she remarked on his sallow complexion and filthy appearance, he replied, "Ah, that is because of the wolf's skin I wear."

Gloatingly—his clumsy wooing apparently forgotten—Grenier told her that a man named Pierre Labouriat had given him the pelt and he regularly put it on before 'haunting' the woods and fields as a wolf. There were nine such wolves in his 'coven', he said, who went to the chase at the waning of the moon on Mondays, Fridays and Saturdays during the twilight and just before dawn.

Warming to his grisly subject, Grenier said he lusted for the flesh of young children, which was "tender, plump and rare." In wolf's shape, he had often killed dogs and lapped their hot blood, though it did not appeal to his taste as much as the blood of young boys, from whose thighs he had bitten "huge hunks of flesh."

The magistrate was appalled at the

The dreaded Wild Beast of Gevaudin. It could paralyze with a blow of its tail, and terrorized 18th-century France. Below: the werewolf seen in human and equally destructive form.

story, yet he still clung to the rational explanation that Grenier may merely have been boorishly trying to impress the girl with a horror story. He was soon disabused of the idea. When questioned, Grenier unhesitatingly admitted the attack on Marguerite Poirier, adding that but for her stick he would have torn her limb from limb as he had "already eaten three or four children."

Grenier was immediately arrested and at his High Court trial on June 2, 1603, he freely confessed what was described at the time as "the most abominable and hideous werewolfery." The court shuddered—maybe with the realization that it could have happened to any one of them—when Grenier described how he had been 'initiated' into the cult of the werewolf. He had been in the depths of the forest, with another youth named Pierre de la Tilhaire, when a tall, dark stranger appeared, dressed all in black and riding a black charger, who presented each of them with a wolf skin. When they put on the skin, they seemed to be instantly transformed into wolves and in this shape they ravaged the countryside. Before putting on the skin they covered themselves with an oint-

ment—a frequent practice of werewolves. Both were told never to pare the nail of the left thumb, which had to grow thick and crooked like a claw.

Grenier's own accounts of his attacks on children were confirmed by the parents of the victims. But there was no sign of the other youth who had prowled alongside Grenier on his murderous forays. Pierre de la Tilhaire was never found, despite intensive searches by the authorities. Since the attacks did not recur, de la Tilhaire was believed to have died in his 'wolf's lair'.

On September 6, 1603, Grenier was sentenced at the Parliament of Bordeaux. His penalty was remarkably lenient. Taking into consideration his "youth and extreme ignorance," President Dassis ordered him to be confined for life in the strict Franciscan Friary of St Michael the Archangel in Bordeaux, with the warning that any attempt to escape would be punished by his death

on the gallows.

The *loup garou*—as the werewolf was known through France—was incarcerated in a monastic cell where, seven years later, a visitor found him to be "a lean and gaunt lad with small, deep-set eyes that glared fiercely, long sharp teeth like fangs and hands that were almost like claws."

Grenier clearly still felt the 'call' of the wolfskin. He repeatedly fell on all fours in front of his visitor, moving with unusual agility. But he only had another year to live in this lamentable state. He died in November 1611.

Jean Grenier, although certainly a murderer, would today be considered a sufferer from lycanthropy, a psychiatric state in which a person believes he is a wolf or some other non-human animal; such as the bear in Europe, Northern Asia and North America, the hyena or leopard in Africa, and the tiger in India, China, Japan and other parts of Asia.

Stories of men turning into beasts are found in the literature of ancient Greece, and the superstition dates from even earlier times. Some werewolves —the word derives from the old English *wer* or man, and means man-wolf—were believed to be able to change shape at will. Others, in whom the condition was hereditary or acquired by having been bitten by a werewolf, changed shape involuntarily under the influence of a full moon. Among the many significant 'symptoms' of werewolf possession is dryness of the tongue and an inordinate thirst. Both these conditions are a feature of the dreadful disease known as rabies, which can be passed to humans by infected dogs, wolves or foxes. Other symptoms of rabies are muscular contraction—causing the victim to crouch—and a kind of hoarse barking. It is easy to see the effect the sudden appearance of a rabies sufferer would have on superstitious minds . . . particularly if, at the same time, there were a sadistic murderer or even a dangerous wolf on the prowl. Similar physical effects were suffered by early witches who drugged themselves with hyoscyamine (henbane) or stramonium to produce soaring and flying hallucinations.

For centuries, werewolves were commonly believed to be sorcerers. They became wolves by applying an ointment to their naked bodies or by putting on a magic girdle given to them by the Devil or a demon. After death, they were said to become vampires, thereby joining the ranks of the undead.

Theologians in the Middle Ages, when belief in werewolves was widespread, debated whether the man-turned-into-beast could still retain remnants of his humanity. If anyone doubted whether a man could take the shape of a beast, he was promptly referred to the fourth chapter of the Book of Daniel, which tells how the great King Nebuchadnezzar "did eat grass as oxen, and his body was wet with the dew of heaven, till his hairs were grown like eagles' feathers and his nails like birds' claws."

Jean Grenier, who was probably mentally retarded, was treated with rare humanity. Elsewhere in Europe, convicted lycanthropes were lucky to be burned alive. Germany's most notorious werewolf, Peter Stump (or Stumpf, Stube, Stubbe, Sub as the name is spelt in varying accounts), endured a penalty almost as atrocious as his own crimes.

During a rampage lasting 25 years, Stump killed 13 children, two women and one man in the area of Bedburg, near Cologne. The two women he killed were pregnant. He tore the children out of the wombs and ate their hearts "panting hotte and raw." As well as killing countless lambs and kids, eating their

raw flesh, he was alleged to have killed and eaten his son while in the guise of a wolf and also to have committed incest with his daughter. Stump's fearful reign of terror ended when a wolf which had been pursued by men and dogs apparently changed before the eyes of the hunters into human shape. Stump was then seized and taken to jail.

At his trial in 1589, Stump told the magistrates how the Devil had given him a girdle which, when he put it on,

Hirsutism, excessive growth of hair on the body, seen in a werewolf film left, could be one natural explanation for the myths that have abounded since ancient times. Rabies, lycanthropy and doses of hyoscyamine could be other sources of the werewolf stories which took such strong hold in Europe. (Below) A 17th-century werewolf meets its grisly end.

had turned him into a wolf. The girdle was never recovered, the authorities concluding that the Devil had somehow reclaimed it.

With cold legal ferocity, Stump was sentenced to have his body broken on a wheel, his flesh pulled from his bones with red-hot pincers, his legs and arms to be broken with a wooden axe and his head to be struck from his body, which was then to be consigned to the flames. Sadly, this ruthless judgment extended to both the woman with whom Stump lived and his daughter, who were regarded as accomplices in his crimes. They were "burned quicke to ashes" when Stump's sentence was carried out.

The French *loup garou,* Gilles Garnier —who had been executed at Lyons only 16 years earlier—told a similar story about being 'seduced' by a devil. Garnier confessed that one evening he made a pact with a phantom whom he had encountered in a remote and haunted spot in the forest. This phantom, he said, deluded him with fine promises and taught him how to become a wolf by the application of an ointment. Garnier said he had killed and eaten several children while in the shape of a wolf and although he was convicted of "the most hideous sorceries," modern observers regard it as significant that he was in *human* form when he was caught just after strangling a young boy.

The Wild Beast

France, indeed, has had more than its fair share of werewolves. During 1764-65, a monster known as the Wild Beast of Gevaudan spread panic through the entire Languedoc region. The creature was supposed by some to be a panther or hyena; others said it was the offspring of a tiger and a lioness. Countryfolk in the Gevaudan district were convinced that the monster was a warlock who had undergone a transformation and that it was useless to try to catch him. One farmer, a wealthy and much-respected man, testified before a magistrate that when he met the beast it made a prodigious bound through the air and "boasted of the leap in human tones." Eventually after devouring more than a hundred people—the beast was killed, though it stubbornly refused to resume human shape. The exact identity of the creature is still unknown.

Although Britain appeared to have been safe from the menace—and, significantly, free of rabies—a man named Saunderson who hid in a cave in Ben MacDhui, in the Scottish Cairngorms, was thought to be a werewolf. Saunderson, who lived in the 18th-century, was even believed to be descended from a whole line of werewolves and accounts describe his "evil leerie eyes and eyebrows that meet in a point over his

nose." Such eyebrows are said to be a mark of the werewolf, along with extreme hideousness, strong and claw-like fingernails and pointed or small, flat ears.

20th-Century Werewolf

According to legend, a werewolf could only be killed by a silver bullet and a story long believed in the English Channel Islands tells how a Mr Le Marchant often fired at a marauding white rabbit until one day, he detached a silver button, took specially-careful aim and pressed the trigger. The rabbit immediately disappeared behind a hedge. Mr Le Marchant ran to the other side and found a woman neighbor lying with her leg broken and bleeding profusely from a fresh wound. A similar tale from the forest regions of Transylvania, now part of Rumania, describes how a large wolf attacked a woman while she was making hay. While she fought off the animal, she shouted for her husband, who eventually appeared from the forest—but only after the wolf had gone.

His presence wasn't altogether a relief. For she noticed that he still had in his teeth a piece of cloth which matched that torn from her apron by the wolf. She realized that she was married to a werewolf.

Belief in the werewolf is an expression

of the terror felt for centuries of the most dreaded beast in the forest. The werewolf in earlier centuries was often a rapist or murderer—some bands of forest bandits dressed in wolfskins to terrify passers-by—but now the monster lurks in the depths of the mind, symbolic of the beast that is in all of us.

It was this terrifying creature of the imagination which lunged to the surface on July 14, 1949, when a police patrol in central Rome heard howls coming from the bushes of a garden late at night. Under the full moon, they found Pasquale Rosini, covered in mud, digging in the ground with his fingernails and howling. In hospital, Rosini said that for three years he had regularly lost consciousness at periods of full moon and had found himself wandering the streets at night "driven by uncontrollable instincts." He was sent to a clinic for observation.

Treatment unfortunately came too late to save another victim, 17-year-old Andrew Prinold, of Staffordshire, England, who confided to a friend that his hands and face were changing color. Then he began growling. The youth was later found in a pool of blood with his own flick-knife lying partly open near him. On April 28, 1975, an inquest jury returned a verdict of suicide on the boy who believed he was "a werewolf of the seventies."

The 16th-century German werewolf Peter Stump claimed at his trial to have been given a magic belt by the Devil which changed him into a werewolf, but his captors could not find it. His reign of terror lasted for 25 years in which he killed 13 children and three adults. This contemporary pamphlet shows his capture and final agonizing death. In the film *I Was a Teenage Werewolf* Michael Landon (below) shows the effects of hirsutism.

Ronald Grant

THE COFFINS HAVE MOVED AGAIN!

Every time they opened the vault, it was the same macabre story. The heavy coffins had been strewn about like matchboxes. As fear and hysteria mounted, the Governor of the island ordered the vault to be sealed. Then came reports of 'unearthly scufflings' inside and once more the tomb had to be opened. What they saw made the workmen drop their tools and take to their heels.

Everyone who attended the funeral said the same—it was the most extraordinary and significant such event in the history of Barbados. The remains of a worthy but unimportant white woman, Mrs. Thomasina Clarke, were escorted to their final resting-place by a procession of hundreds, headed by the Governor of the island, Lord Combermere, and his staff. Solemnly, on horse, on foot, and by carriage the mourners journeyed from Bridgetown, the capital, to the graveyard of Christ Church, eight miles away on Oistin Bay. There lay the vault which had caused so much controversy and fear. And it was because of the weird happenings in the Chase Vault—named after one of the island's most distinguished families—that Lord Combermere felt he should be present at the burial.

Although the vault had, in the past, mainly been reserved for the Chases, it was agreed that others could be interred in it. Friends of the family or those whose bereaved relatives had made a touching request. In fact, the first person to be put to rest there—12 years earlier in 1807—had not been a Chase at all. The corpse of Mrs. Thomasina Goddard, an intimate of the family's, had been placed there as a mark of regard.

The vault, measuring some 12 feet by 7, was considered a fine place for the deceased. Imbedded in limestone rock, it was made of large blocks of coral stone firmly cemented together. From the outside, the tall arched roof appeared to be flat and the entrance was discreetly set in one of the sides. The door consisted of a heavy chunk of solid marble, and it took a team of muscular laborers to open and close it.

Sudden Death

Half-a-dozen negro workmen were needed to seal in Mrs. Goddard—the first occupant—and she was not officially disturbed until the following February, when two-year-old Mary Anna Chase was placed beside her. Four years passed and then Mary Anna's elder sister, Dorcas, also expired and was laid in the vault. Then, just a month later, in August 1812, yet another Chase died.

This time it was the turn of the Honorable Thomas Chase, the dead girls' father, to be put in an expensive, lead-lined coffin and buried with full pomp and ceremony. A huge, coarse figure weighing more than 240 pounds, Chase had been a notorious bully and womanizer and was felt to be no great loss to Barbados. Nevertheless, scores of people made the pilgrimage to Christ Church to see him put underground.

It was then, as a squad of negroes prized back the marble door, that the first sensation occurred. As the stone was pulled aside, and sunlight streamed

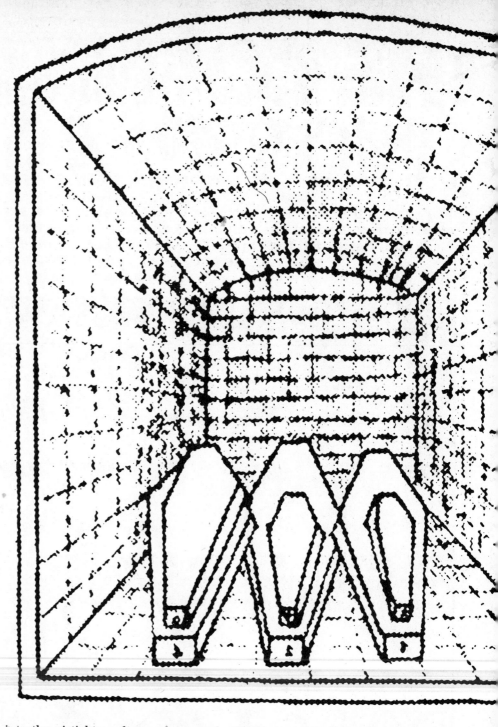

into the airtight vault, people started forward to peer inside. Those at the front suddenly gasped and then froze in horror. Instead of the three previous coffins being neatly in line, they had been *moved out of place.* That of Mrs. Goddard was lying on its side against a wall. That of Mary Anna Chase had been toppled disrespectfully into a corner. That of Dorcas Chase had been turned completely upside down.

It seemed as if some of the islanders —white or black—had broken into the vault and caused the disruption. But what possible motive could such vandals have? Stifling their curiosity, the onlookers allowed the burial to go ahead. Later, however, back in Bridgetown,

there was no other topic of conversation. Barbados is a small place—21 miles long and 14 miles across—and before long everyone was discussing the bizarre goings-on and putting forward theories.

Treasure-hunting pirates was among the least grotesque of these. But it soon emerged that there was a link between the four corpses now in the vault—one which, in the circumstances, was stronger than blood or mere friendship. Each of the deceased—Mrs. Goddard, Mary Anna, Dorcas, and Thomas Chase—had died suddenly and from no apparent cause. It was whispered that they had all been murdered, poisoned by someone who had a grudge against the Chase family and their associates.

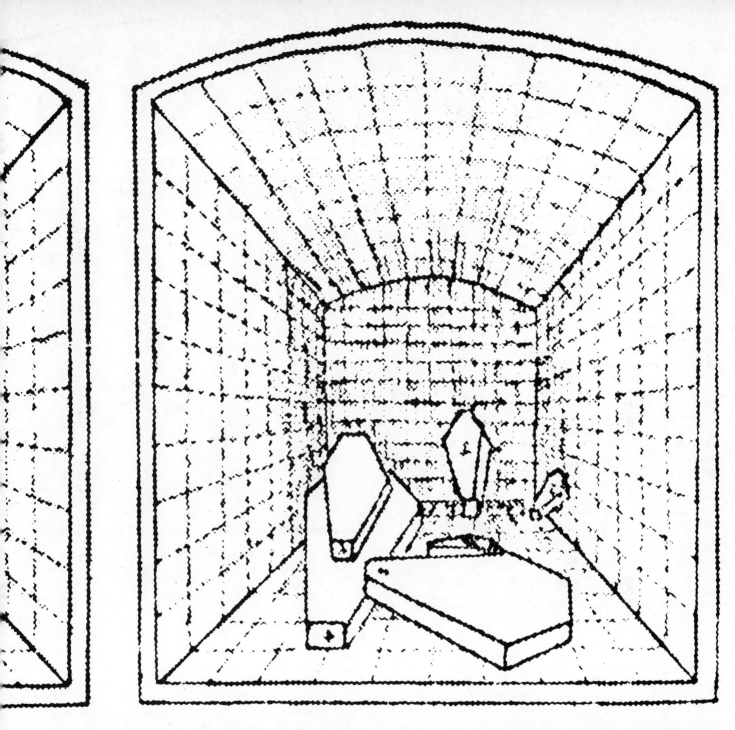

However, there the conjecture ended. There was no obvious suspect and the puzzle of the displaced or 'moving' coffins stayed unsolved. It wasn't until September 1816 that the talk started up again. Yet another person connected with the Chases had died—little Samuel Brewster Ames, aged 11 months. Once more no definite cause of death had been established. According to the Ames's doctor, the baby had been 'too weak' to survive. At the request of the infant's parents, Samuel was not to have an 'ordinary' grave. He was to enter the Chase Vault and to lie there in 'splendor'.

The majority of those who attended the funeral were sensation-seekers. They were not disappointed. As the vault was opened for the first time in four years everyone craned forward to see or hear about what, if anything, had happened inside. At the time of the Hon. Thomas's burial all four coffins had been reverently lined-up. But now there was again chaos in the vault—with the coffins turned over and thrown about as if they had been matchboxes.

Once again they were put straight and young Samuel's body was placed beside them. After that there was no stopping the rumors, which spread throughout the entire British West Indies. Journalists and sightseers came to the island and one reporter wrote, "The moving of these heavy, lead-encased coffins is undoubtedly the work of black magic, of

The position of the coffins (left) when the vault was sealed in 1819 and when it was opened the next year.

Voodoo. In my view, Voodoo witch doctors have been at work and are, for some unknown reason, taking vengeance on the souls of those buried in Chase Vault."

The vault was again shut up, but no special guard was placed over it. There was no investigation into the activities of local medicine-men or criminals, and the newspaperman concluded, "From all this it would appear that Lord Combermere does not want to clash or interfere with forces outside his own rational understanding. It could be said that he was afraid if he was not known to be a man of honor and courage."

Meanwhile, the negroes boycotted Christ Church and could only be made to work there under severe threats. The white residents of the West Indies, however, were less superstitious and fearful. They arrived from Jamaica and as far away as British Honduras, on the Central American mainland, and according to the parish clerk at Christ Church were completely lacking in Christian decorum and decency. "They appeared," he stated, "to regard that portion of hallowed ground as no better than a bull pit or a puppet show, with the advantage that it did not cost them a cent."

It was obvious that many people were hoping for more occult happenings in the graveyard and so, when the funeral of Mrs. Thomasina Clarke was arranged —in July 1819—Lord Combermere decided to inspect the vault for himself. He and his entourage stood apprehensively by as yet again the workmen opened the chamber. The Governor was the first person to look inside it, and for once the former cavalry officer and scourge of the French in 1808, during the Peninsular War, felt his blood chill.

It seemed as if a bunch of lunatics had been set loose in the vault. Splintered and dented, the coffins looked as if they had been dashed about for sport. It was only the lead lining that had prevented the skeletons from tumbling onto the stone floor. This time the Governor did demand action. Once the coffins had again been put in their proper place and order, and that of Mrs. Clarke's set with them, he ordered that sand should be strewn on the ground and that the door should be cemented shut. While the cement was still wet he and some of his staff pressed their seals into it.

Unearthly Scufflings

Seven months passed and periodic checks showed that the seals were still unbroken. However, there was talk of strange noises at night in the graveyard and of 'unearthly scufflings' inside the chamber. The stories became so hysterical that Lord Combermere held a meeting at his residence on April 18, 1820, to discuss this latest development. There was only one way to stop the panic talk, he declared, and that was to reopen the tomb. So, later that day, he and his aides once more set off for Christ Church.

As expected, the seals had not been tampered with and there were no pick or chisel marks on the cement around the marble door. It took the natives longer than ever to chip and force the door open and once they'd done so they dropped their tools and fled. It was as well for them that they did. For, inside, the vault was a shambles. The coffins were in total disarray and, strangest and most frightening of all, there were no footprints in

Viscount Combermere, Governor of Barbados, inspected the Chase Vault and found the coffins scattered.

the white Barbados sand. The vault and its surroundings were thoroughly searched, but no clue was found.

"I examined the walls, the arch, and every part of the vault," wrote the Hon. Nathan Lucas, one of those present, later. "A mason in my presence struck every part of the bottom with his hammer, and all was solid. I confess myself at a loss to account for the movements of these leaden coffins. Thieves certainly had no hand in it; and as for any practical wit or hoax, too many were requisite to be trusted with the secret for it to remain unknown; and as for negroes having anything to do with it, their superstitious fear of the dead and everything belonging to them precludes any idea of the kind. All I know is that it happened and that I was an eye-witness."

This time Lord Combermere had experienced enough. He no longer cared whether the desecrators were human or otherwise. He ordered the removal of the five coffins and made arrangements for them to be reburied in another part of the churchyard. Officially, the affair was at an end. But it didn't stop psychic

investigators from probing the mystery.

Chief amongst these in later years was Sir Arthur Conan Doyle, the creator of Sherlock Holmes, and an obsessive believer in spiritualism and life after death. He spent the last 15 years of his life, from 1915 onwards, seeking an answer to the all-important question, "Does death end all?" Regarding the macabre occurrences in the Chase Vault he had a theory . . .

He believed, as had many of the islanders, that all those buried in the vault had not met natural deaths. For one reason or another they had been murdered, three of them at early ages. This, therefore, brought about what Doyle called 'effluvium'—a mysterious substance which, he said, sometimes forms after death, especially in the case of young people, and which has a 'combustion effect' upon the atmosphere. It was this 'unused vitality' emanating from the bodies which made the coffins move.

Today, despite a hurricane which devastated the churchyard in 1831, and a fire which destroyed the rebuilt church itself in 1935, the Chase Vault still exists. People are no longer buried in it, and it is now just a monument to what Conan Doyle would have called The Strange Case of the Moving Coffins.

THE CURSE OF THE KENNEDYS

This is the 'Golden Family', blessed by wealth and touched by genius. Nothing seems beyond the grasp of the Kennedys. Power, prestige and an almost legendary glamor are all theirs. Yet a malign influence dogs their every step, striking unerringly at the peak of their triumphs.

success and happiness seem assured.

For generations they have been a family with everything life can promise within their reach, yet haunted constantly by sudden death and sorrow. It has transformed the glorious Kennedy dream into a Greek tragedy.

Nobody knows how it began, this burden of disaster, but it has been passed on down through the generations of Kennedys like some terrifying, indestructible heirloom. Certainly when Joseph P. Kennedy, John's father, married Rose Fitzgerald in Boston on October 7, 1914, tragedy had already entered their lives.

Rose's only sister, Eunice, had died of tuberculosis at the age of 23, apparently contracted when she was doing Red Cross work during World War I. Joseph's only brother died in infancy.

In Ireland, where superstition is a way of life, it might have been taken as an omen. In the brave new world of America, where the couple's families had settled, it seemed nothing more than a sad coincidence.

Joseph Kennedy was an ambitious man. He hungered for money, power, success. He achieved them all. He was a bank president at 25, a millionaire before he was 30, film tycoon and high-powered entrepreneur. In 1937 he

At 12.30 pm on Friday November 22, 1963, time stopped for President John F. Kennedy. On Main Street in Dallas, Texas, out of the midst of a friendly crowd, an assassin's bullet from a $21 rifle found its mark, and the world wept.

For the 24-year-old murderer, Lee Harvey Oswald, it meant an infamous place in the history books. For America it meant the end of their fairy-tale President, their dream of Camelot. For the Kennedys it was yet one more tragic example of the curse that hangs menacingly over their family; a curse that consistently shadows triumph with tragedy, that strikes viciously whenever

Rose Kennedy with her first three children, Joe Jr., Rosemary and JFK. (Right) The family circle: Patricia on the arm of her father's chair, JFK behind, Jean, 9, and Eunice, 16, in front. Behind Mrs. Kennedy is Joseph Jr., Rosemary, 19, Robert, 12, Kathleen, 17, and Edward beside his mother.

became the first Irish Catholic to be American ambassador to Britain.

And like so many men who have achieved success themselves, he was anxious for glory for his children. Glory and power. "The measure of a man's success in life is not the money he's made. It's the kind of family he's raised," said Joe. And *his* family was like nobody else's.

True, he arranged for each of his nine children to have $1 million at the age of 21. But, despite this, through a freak combination of genes, minds, upbringing and sheer energy, they were able to achieve what no American family had ever achieved before. But at a price so high that it seemed as if fate had made a deal with the devil himself.

Nine months after Rose and Joe's Boston society wedding—which marked the union of two politically ambitious Irish clans—their first son, Joseph P. Jr., was born. Two years later John F. arrived, followed after another two years by a daughter, Rosemary. But already, unbeknown to them, the family had been touched by tragedy . . .

Joe and Rose were delighted with their pretty baby daughter. She had a sweet temperament and cried less than the boys. Her mother assumed it was because she was a girl that her progress was slower than her brothers'. Rosemary learned to crawl later than the boys, had difficulty with childish games, such as steering a sled, and great trouble trying to read and write.

Eventually her parents learned the heartbreaking truth. Their sunny little daughter was mentally retarded. "Rosemary's was the first of the tragedies that were to befall us," says her mother.

In the early 'twenties, little was known about the mentally deficient. Rather than put her into an institution the Kennedys decided to bring Rosemary up at home. They kept her condition a close family secret and lavished on her love and encouragement.

Win, Win, Win

For 22 years, Rosemary stayed with them, indulged and protected by her family, leading a more or less normal life. But then her condition began to deteriorate. She became tense and irritable and inclined to fly into rages. Finally the doctors recommended neurosurgery. The operation eliminated the violence and convulsions but left her permanently mentally incapacitated. Her saddened parents were forced to send her to a convent in Wisconsin where she has been ever since.

Not until 1960, when John was running for President, did her father publicly reveal the truth about Rosemary.

In 1934, Joe and Rose had their ninth and last child, Edward, bringing the total to four sons and five daughters. The children grew up in a strict Catholic environment. Their father indoctrinated them with his own political ambitions, instilled in them the fierce family loyalty that was to stay with them through their triumphs and disasters and, above all, taught them to win, win, win. In athletic sports, in academic stakes, in life. In the Kennedy Clan there was no room for losers.

In this environment, and backed by their heritage of self-determination, the family were destined for success, unaware that disaster would befall them at the moment of their greatest triumphs.

On August 1, 1943, 26-year-old John met with it when he was captain of the PT-109 boat on a wartime mission in the South Pacific. A Japanese destroyer rammed his boat, slicing the 80-foot plywood hull in half, spilling fuel all over the stern. Kennedy was thrown back in the cockpit, ramming his back against a steel frame. The impact crushed one crew member whose body was never found. Another was badly burned.

Eventually the survivors were rescued but John Kennedy was badly hurt, mangled by coral cuts and with back injuries which were to cause him agony for the rest of his life.

One year later, tragedy returned to the Kennedys. This time the victim was their oldest son, Joe, who had been groomed for glory from the day he was born, the one destined to be President.

Rose had a theory about raising children. "The oldest boys usually take more responsibility than the others," she said. "Bring up the oldest one the way you want them all to go."

So that was Joe. The prototype Kennedy, reared to succeed. Dynamic, sociable, easy-going, strong, independent, he possessed all the qualities for greatness.

Twenty-nine years old, a lieutenant in the naval air arm, the only man to volunteer to fly a radio-controlled Liberator bomber loaded with eleven tons of explosive off a secret English airfield, Joe never reached his destination. The plane rose to its appointed height, blew up with a thunderous bang and vanished.

Stricken with grief, Joe Kennedy Sr. told his wife, "We've got to carry on. We must take care of the living. There is a lot of work to be done."

Only three weeks later, the malign influence hovering over the family struck again.

Popperfoto

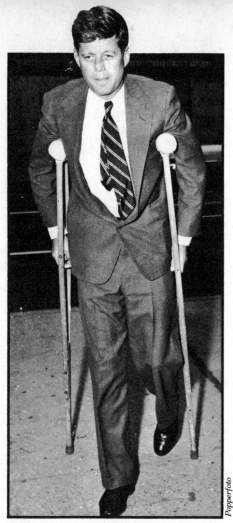

JFK was dogged by ill-health all his life. He regarded the possibility of violent death fatalistically . . . and it came in Dallas.

The Kennedys' fourth child, slim, vivacious Kathleen, had four months earlier married an Englishman, William Cavendish, Marquess of Hartington, against their wishes. Not only was he non-Catholic but his ancestors had for generations held high office in the English government in Ireland, traditionally responsible for suppressing the independence of the Irish. Of the family, only her devoted big brother Joe attended the wedding in England, to give her away.

The newly-weds had just one month together in London before Billy, a Coldstream Guards captain, rejoined his regiment. He was killed while leading a patrol casually across a French battlefield, calling to his men, "Come on, you fellows! Buck up!"

Later Kathleen wrote sadly to a friend, "I guess God has taken care of the problem in His own way, hasn't He?" She stayed on in England, moving in high society, helping to patch up the war wounded, still in touch with her now-remorseful family.

In May 1948, on holiday in the Riviera, she arranged to meet her father in Paris. She flew there with a few friends in a private plane but the weather turned bad and the navigation equipment was inadequate. On Thursday the 13th the plane crashed into a mountainside killing all on board. Joe Kennedy's reunion with his daughter was to watch her body being brought down the mountain in an ox-drawn cart. She had been found by a farmer, thrown clear of the wreckage,

lying on the ground as if asleep.

Already the Kennedy dynasty was being cruelly chipped away. But, for the rest of the family, life went on.

Teddy, the youngest child, born 19 years after his brother Joe, was a freshman at Harvard in 1951. Aware that he was heading for a C-minus grade in Spanish he asked a classmate to take the examination for him. Both students were expelled. "I made a mistake," admitted Teddy. "I was having difficulty in the course."

It was a mistake that caused more pain to his bitterly disappointed father. No Kennedy ever cheated—or, indeed, should ever need to.

With Joe Jr. dead, Mr. Kennedy's ambitions transferred to the next son in line, John. Heir to a dream, he took up the mantle gladly and threw himself into the political career laid down for him by two generations of Kennedys.

$400 Million Backing

Backed by his father's millions (by now Joe Sr. was reputed to be worth more than $400 million) and his family's dedication to the cause, the war hero began his climb to the White House.

His brother, Bobby, nine years his junior, cut his political teeth on Jack's 1946 campaign. In 1952, fresh from the University of Virginia Law School, Bobby brought his own brand of vigor and organization to his brother's crucial campaign to win the Senate seat held by Republican Henry Cabot Lodge, a seat no other Democrat in the state dared challenge.

With his three younger sisters and his mother campaigning on his behalf Jack could hardly fail. He defeated Lodge by just under 80 000 votes to become the highest elected Democrat in his state, with a huge female vote.

Always a lady's man, on September 12, 1953, John F. Kennedy resigned his bachelorhood to marry the beautiful Jacqueline Bouvier.

Touched by the Kennedy bad luck that seems to spill over even into the lives of their in-laws, Jackie had a miscarriage that same year, followed three years later by a stillbirth. Then, in 1957 and 1960 she had a daughter, Caroline and a son, John F. Jr. to the delight of her family-loving husband.

But already the rumors were growing that John and Jackie's marriage was undergoing immense difficulties. For one thing they had little in common. Jackie was in love with the arts while John found culture boring, preferring comedy and musicals to the *avant garde*.

And before long the stories of his affairs with other women kept the gossips happy while his family—particularly his deeply religious mother—attempted to ignore the scandals.

His back still troubled him constantly and frequently forced him to resort to crutches. He had a series of spinal operations but they did little to help. His family went out of their way to conceal the fact that he was born with an unstable back and, indeed, despite his healthy, athletic image, he suffered ill-health for most of his life.

As a child he had scarlet fever and a blood infection; as a schoolboy he suffered from jaundice and appendicitis attacks; and at the end of his first term at Princeton he caught hepatitis.

After the PT-boat incident, a bout of malaria reduced him to a weak 120 pounds and returned to plague him regularly. Four times his family sat by his death bed only to have him pull through yet another drama.

Only in recent years was it learned that John F. Kennedy suffered from Addison's Disease—an insufficiency of the production of hormones by the adrenal cortex—and was kept alive by drugs for the last 15 years of his life. Ironically, the cortisone may have been responsible for Kennedy's air of youthful vigor and vitality and may also have increased his notorious sexual desire.

Camelot Dream

Had the public been aware he had the disease it is quite likely he would never have become President. As it was, on January 20, 1961, in a snow-clad Washington, John F. Kennedy was inaugurated as President of the United States, after narrowly beating Richard Nixon. He had fulfilled his father's dream. Now he set about building his own Camelot.

Under his leadership the White House took on the very atmosphere of a court, complete with courtiers, liegemen and fools. President John Kennedy was enchanted by his own version of the original court of King Arthur—reflecting the romantic attitudes of the Lerner and Loewe musical.

Every night before he went to sleep he would play the film's soundtrack and his favorite lines were

> *'Don't let it be forgot*
> *That once there was a spot*
> *For one brief shining moment*
> *That was known as Camelot.'*

He surrounded himself with the cream of the world's statesmen and celebrities and became the darling of American society. He entertained a stream of beautiful women in the Lincoln bedroom of the White House whenever Jackie was traveling in Europe or vacationing in Florida. He was regarded as the political Messiah his country had awaited.

His father was overjoyed that the glory he had sought for his family was finally theirs. But, as had been proved so often, the Kennedys could overcome any obstacle but their destiny. And, once again, destiny was poised to strike.

Joe Kennedy had never really recovered from his oldest son's death. In December 1961, aged 73, he was out playing golf at the Palm Beach Country Club with his niece Ann Gargan when he announced, "I don't really feel well today, but it must be the cold I've had."

He was taken home and then rushed to St Mary's Hospital where it was found that a stroke had paralyzed his right side. It was the end of an era for the indomitable Kennedy patriarch. He never recovered his power to speak or walk. The right side of his body withered. The only word he could say was 'no'.

Nonetheless he could still read the papers and enjoy the company of his family. And he still followed avidly the

Popperfoto

President's political progress.

On August 7, 1963, Jackie Kennedy gave birth to a third child, Patrick, nearly six weeks prematurely. Almost immediately the doctors noticed that the baby had difficulty in breathing and he was placed in an oxygen chamber. President Kennedy raced to the hospital along with brothers Bobby and Ted and sister Jean.

Bowed with worry, John Kennedy strode up and down the hospital corridors trailed by his secret service men and the press. For two days he kept vigil and then, less than 40 hours old, Patrick Bouvier Kennedy died.

He was buried by Cardinal Cushing, a close friend of the Kennedys, who had married Jackie and John. Later Cardinal Cushing said of the President, "He wouldn't take his hands off of that little coffin. I was afraid he'd carry it right out with him."

The Assassination

John F. Kennedy himself once said, "It is against the law of nature for parents to bury their children." Tragically, it was something that was to happen to his own father four times.

And so the curse flourished; unremitting, unexplained. With joy came inevitable disaster—so often death, lurking silently, violent. It had become so much a way of life that the family were almost numbed to the shock, immune to the pain.

Thus, on November 22, 1963, when the first radio reports came through from Dallas that someone had taken some shots at the President, Rose Kennedy greeted them with mixed reactions.

John had survived so many times before that he seemed indestructible. Surely this time it could not be that serious; some more hard luck, perhaps; another problem with his health, another set-back to surmount.

In her own book, *Times to Remember*, Rose confesses, ". . . I had trained myself through the years not to become too visibly upset at bad news, even very bad news, because I had a strong notion that if I broke down, everybody else in the household would." This time it *was* very bad news.

In the open-topped presidential Lincoln, John F. Kennedy had ridden triumphantly through the streets of Dallas, stopping continually to shake hands with the excited crowd. Governor John Connally of Texas sat in the front with his wife who had turned round to say: "Mr President, you can't say Dallas doesn't love you."

Seconds later the shots rang out. Kennedy lurched forward and grabbed his neck. There were shouts of "The President's been hit!" A 6.5 millimeter bullet had entered the back of Kennedy's neck, bruised his right lung, ripped his wind-

November 25, 1963 and Jacqueline Kennedy leaves the Capitol for the funeral of her President-husband. She is flanked by brothers-in-law Teddy (right) and Robert—next in line for glory . . . and for death.

pipe and gone out again through his throat, passing through Governor Connally's back, chest, right wrist and left thigh. But it was not the bullet that killed the President. That came seconds later and took off the top of his head.

One hour and twenty minutes later, after killing a police officer, Lee Harvey Oswald was caught. "Everybody will know who I am now," he told a police captain proudly. But his heroics were short lived. Two days later Lee Harvey Oswald was killed himself, shot by a stunted strip club boss, Jack Ruby, who thought he owed it to his country. He fired at Oswald in the jail garage as the President's assassin was being transfered to another prison. It was all over.

The Golden Boy of the Kennedy Legend was dead. Murdered by a distorted little man with a cheap rifle, taken abruptly from his Camelot by yet another twist of the fate that had dogged his family for so long. John F. Kennedy's one brief shining moment was over.

To his countrymen President Kennedy was the victim of a peculiar national accident. To those who were closest to him he was a victim of his birth, and the inexplicable curse that went with it.

"If someone is going to kill me, they are going to kill me," he said only hours before he was shot.

Later Jackie was to admit, "The poignancy of men dying young haunted him." As President he spoke often of the possibility of death, but never anxiously. He regarded it almost fatalistically, seeming to recognize that his only enemy was time.

He had reigned as President for a little over one thousand days, long enough to make an indelible mark on history. He was 46 when he died in Jackie's arms on that legendary motorcade to nowhere.

The malign curse, one would have thought, might now have been satisfied; its awful appetite sated. But not only did the Curse of the Kennedys live on, it gathered heartbreaking new strength.

The Mythmakers

'Aaargh, the monster's got me!'

Carnivorous vegetables, homicidal plants, lethal lumps of metal-piping and faceless fiends. They all sprang from the imaginations of SF artists searching for the ideal Thing from Outer Space.

Scientifiction by

A. Hyatt Verrill

David H. Keller, M.D.

Miles J. Breuer, M.D.

THE BEST IN SCIENCE FICTION

Anthony Frewin

It must have been something he drank. What else but an alcoholic nightmare could explain the experience of the solitary boozer on the cover of *Wonder Stories* of June 1935 . . . suddenly attacked by perambulating vegetables from another planet?

What else, in fact, but the burgeoning imagination of the science fiction illustrators and artists, seeking ever more horrific ways of depicting alien creatures from the cosmos.

In their search for the ideal 'Little Green Man', artists have visualized aliens in every possible animal, vegetable and mineral form.

Until relatively recently, they all had one thing in common: they meant nothing but trouble to the human race.

The worried-looking Martians filing out of their spacecraft in Hans Wessolowski's June 1932 cover for *Amazing Stories* are very much the exception.

1932: "Are the natives friendly?"
1935: vegetables' vengeance.

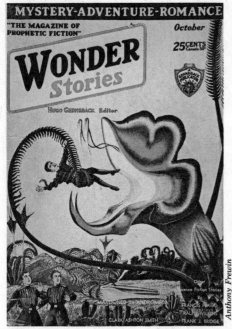

Looking rather like budget-conscious tourists who have landed in an unfamiliar European country and don't trust the water, the Martians' outsize ears already appear to be tuned to listen for a distinctly unfriendly welcome.

Much more in the 'Aaaargh, it's got me!' mold is Frank Paul's man-eating plant busily enjoying its breakfast on *Wonder Stories'* cover of October 1930.

As if the creature (a denizen, apparently, of Andromeda) isn't nasty enough, a caption inside points out, "The strength of the monster may be gauged by the size of the flying creature now dead upon the ground!"

But menace, as many artists soon discovered, can be created by much simpler methods than slapping the color on carnivorous vegetables or providing plants with homicidal digestive systems.

The unnerving boiler-with-legs conjured up by Morey for *Amazing Stories* in April 1938 manages to convey instant doom with the minimum of gore. So do Howard Brown's 'Invaders'—brutal and relentless in their very facelessness —who are about to wreak some fate worse than death on the girl in the 1935 *Astounding Stories* picture. Her companion remains powerless (a familiar figment of real-life nightmare), gripped by a creature who seems to be saying, "Sorry, pal; this hurts me more than it hurts you."

The same brand of inhumanity is hinted at in the tubular creature from Jupiter dreamed up by Wesso for *Astounding Science Fiction* in March 1938. All the Earthman wants to do is to hotfoot downtown for a slice of the action. But no; the soulless alien wraps him in a four-arm lock and the party is clearly over.

Earthman in the clutches of Alien —whatever its shape or size—was the stock *motif* of SF art in the 1930s. But even more horrors were to be faced (and imaginations stretched) before the 'natives' started to get friendly.

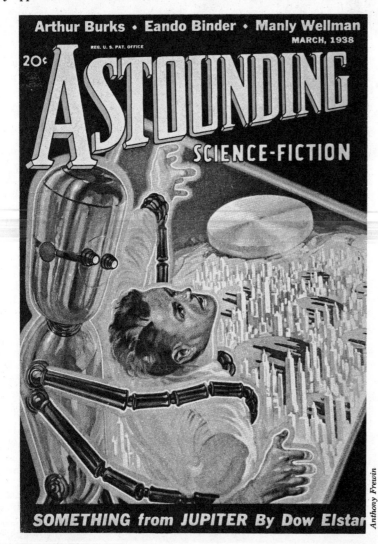

**1930: botanical beast of Andromeda.
1938: a more mechanical menace.
1935: the inhumanity of 'non-humans'.
1938: judo with a thing from Jupiter.**

EMPRESS WHO ONLY WANTED A BABY

Lovely Empress Soraya of Persia had all a woman could desire . . . a rich and noble husband, the affection of her people, wonderful clothes and jewels. Yet her inability to produce a male heir to the Peacock Throne was to wreck her marriage and send her into exile.

Keystone

Popperfoto

On the morning of December 8, 1954, the Empress Soraya of Persia—one of the world's most beautiful, rich, and, it seemed, happy young wives—entered New York's Presbyterian Medical Center for a complete physical check. It was to be the most important such examination of her life, one that could decide her entire personal and marital future. For, at the age of 22, it was thought that Soraya was sterile and could not provide a son to succeed to the throne.

She had been married to the Shah of Persia for almost four years and, so far, had shown no sign of becoming pregnant. This was more serious than she imagined at the time—although her husband knew that it might mean the shock and humiliation of divorce. Her barrenness could become a political issue, with the Prime Minister insisting that an heir be produced—or else.

That Christmas the 'or else' was too unpleasant to think about, and the Shah was overjoyed when—after dozens of long and exhaustive tests—doctors at the Center declared that, physically, there was nothing wrong with Soraya. "She is in fine health and has her best and most fruitful years ahead of her," he was told. "Be patient and children will come."

So the 34-year-old Shah and his radiant Empress returned to Teheran, the capital of Persia, and prepared themselves for the event which they now felt was only a short time away. However, months passed . . . another three years went by . . . and still Soraya was without a child.

It was then, in the winter of 1957, that the ultimatum the Shah most feared was delivered. The country's Premier, after consulting the cabinet, told the monarch that the Empress must present him "with an heir in the near future, or the dynasty's future must be assured in some other way."

Realizing that Soraya would probably never have children, the Shah sought an alternative solution. According to an edict laid down by his late father, no one descended from the Persian Kadshar family could succeed to the throne. This meant that none of the Shah's half-brothers could take his place as ruler as they all had Kadshar mothers.

Unless the ban could be lifted the Shah's marriage was doomed. Soraya now appreciated this and told her heartsick husband "There will be no alternative left to us but to part." In a desperate attempt to prevent this, the Shah appealed to the Council of Wise Men to overrule his father's decree.

To allow the Wise Men time to reach a decision—and to escape from her numerous enemies at court—Soraya decided to leave Persia for a while. So, on February

Popperfoto

13, 1958—the day after their seventh wedding anniversary—the Shah accompanied her to Teheran airport, where he saw her onto a plane for Switzerland.

With his ministers in attendance, and a guard of honor lined up, the Shah waved goodbye to his dark-haired, dark-eyed wife. A cold wind whipped across the tarmac as the plane took off, and both he and Soraya knew that they might never see each other again.

Day after day, Soraya waited in the skiing resort of St. Moritz while the Wise Men deliberated for hour upon hour. Two and then three weeks passed and the Shah spoke to Soraya several times on the telephone. Each time there was no news, and each time he seemed to detect a note of growing despair in her husband's voice.

Meanwhile, as the council still debated the fateful question, people throughout the world curiously awaited the outcome. Newspapers and magazines in most countries retold the story of the 'fairy-tale romance' which now looked like turning into a drama of heartbreak, divorce and loneliness.

Mohamed Reza Pahlavi, Shah of Persia since 1941, was 30 when he first saw two photographs of Soraya Esfandiary taken on a skiing holiday in Switzerland. At the time the monarch had recovered from the bitter experience of his first marriage—to Princess Fawzieh, sister of King Farouk of Egypt. She had borne him a daughter, Princess Shahnaz, but their nine-year union ended in divorce in 1948.

In the two years since then he had been on the look-out for a new bride—someone with looks, breeding, and the ability to produce the son he and his country needed. News of his 'quest' circulated in Europe and came to the ears of Soraya's cousin, Gudars Bahktiary. It was he who showed the two snapshots to the Shah and recommended the 18-year-old beauty as a potential Empress.

The ruler made his own enquiries about the girl, who was still a student, and was pleased with what he learnt. She was the daughter of a Persian diplomat and his German wife and had been born in the Persian textile town of Isfahan. But apart from her name—which meant 'Seven Stars' —there was nothing of the provincial Middle Easterner about her. Her mother had seen to that.

Determined that Soraya would not be forced into a veiled, submissive and sheltered life—a mixture of plaything and slave to the man who deigned to marry her—she took her daughter to Berlin. At the age of only eight months, Soraya was subjected to the 'civilizing' atmosphere of the capital's high society.

When she was 15, as was the custom in such circles, she was sent to an exclusive finishing school in Switzerland. And, in the summer of 1950, she went to live and study in London to perfect her English. It was then that her cousin decided to act as a matchmaker, without her knowledge or consent. So, when she was first told of the Shah's romantic interest in her, she was both startled and intrigued.

Up until then the thought of marriage had not seriously occurred to her. She was too busy enjoying herself, growing up, and making friends of her own age. She began to change her mind, however, when the Shah's sister, Princess Shams, came to London—ostensibly for a holiday, but actually to give the teenager a good looking-over and to sound her out about the idea of becoming the female head of Persia.

The Princess was immediately struck by Soraya's charm, poise and perfect manners. She would be a fitting bride for any monarch and Shams eagerly took over the role of matchmaker—dropping heavy hints about the 'ideal life' that awaited the Shah's next wife. "It would be a wonderful thing," she said poin-

(Left) The photograph the Shah fell in love with: Soraya at 18. At 22, though childless, she was radiant—assured of a future baby at a U.S. clinic.

tedly, "if a young girl such as yourself was willing to marry Mohamed Reza and stand regally by his side."

Influenced by such talk, and by the strange feeling that her life was to undergo a vital change, Soraya agreed to visit the Shah on his home ground. "Deep in myself," she wrote later, "I felt I was about to have an extraordinary experience. The feeling struck me as so absurd that I did not dare mention it for fear of appearing ridiculous. Yet the premonitions remained and grew stronger."

Accompanied by her father, she flew to Teheran on October 7, 1950, and went straight from their white-walled villa to have dinner at the Royal Palace with the Shah and his mother, the Dowager Empress. The occasion was stiff with protocol and formality. Soraya was impressed by the way the ruler's half-brothers addressed him as 'Your Majesty', and by his sisters bowing whenever he spoke to them.

Guest of Honor

Court etiquette was observed and Soraya, as the guest of honor, was seated next to her host and potential husband, the Shah. The conversation was kept on a chatty, everyday basis. How did she enjoy the skiing in Switzerland? What were her impressions of London? Scholastically, what was her favorite subject? Did she do much dancing, swimming, riding? Did she play tennis or golf? Had she been fortunate enough yet to glimpse the King of England?

To all these, and other, questions Soraya replied with her usual tact and courtesy. Then, the meal over, she returned to the villa on her own. Her

61

Popperfoto

Brought up in Germany by her sophisticated European mother, Soraya was perfectly at home when she visited Hamburg in 1955 as Empress of Persia.

father stayed behind to talk some more to the dark and hawk-nosed Shah. She was just getting ready for bed when Mr Esfandiary burst excitedly into her room. The Shah wanted to marry her, he declared. What was more, he wanted an answer immediately, that night!

After only one meeting, Soraya had very little to go upon. She was attracted to the ruler and felt she quite liked him. That, counseled her father, was enough. Love would come later, as inevitably and logically as summer followed spring. And, although in fact she spent some time making up her mind, she afterwards wrote that she had agreed to marry her instant suitor "without a second's hesitation."

Her consent was, without delay, relayed to the Shah—and that night, only a few miles apart, the two of them went to bed knowing that nothing would ever be the same for them again. For Mohamed Reza was no playboy king. He took his duties and responsibilities seriously and was deeply concerned about the economic future and growth of his country—and about the still unsolved problems of his poor, backward, and largely illiterate people.

"Don't imagine that I am offering you an easy life," he told her when they met the next day. "My tasks as ruler will partly become yours, and you will find them both strenuous and wearisome." But Soraya, who already felt that spring was giving way to summer, had no fears about the future. She, too, was prepared to put their country and their people first. She, too, would make personal sacrifices for the greater cause of Persia.

At the time, she didn't know how enormous her final sacrifice might have

to be, and looked no further ahead than February 12, 1951—her wedding day. Arranged marriages were not unusual in Moslem countries, but that of the Shah's dwarfed all others before it. It took place in the flower-filled, perfume-bathed Hall of Mirrors at the capital's Golestan Palace. Everything about it was perfect, with the exception of the weather—which was raw and cold.

Soraya was feeling the after-effects of a severe attack of typhoid fever, and to protect herself from the chill she wore a pair of thick woollen stockings beneath her Christian Dior wedding dress—a fabulous affair of tulle and silver brocade weighing more than 40 pounds. Her petticoats were so voluminous that, at first, she was hardly able to walk in them and a lady-in-waiting mercifully cut away 10 yards of the material.

The ceremony was one of devotion and tradition, with the Shah—in the manner of every Persian groom—giving his bride a crystal bowl filled with powdered sugar, a symbol that their married life will be long, happy . . . and that they will be blessed with sons and daughters.

'Prince of Decadence'

However, three days after returning from their honeymoon, the first of their political troubles began. On March 7, 1951, Prime Minister Razmara was assassinated by a group of religious fanatics and his place was taken by a rabid anti-royalist, Mohamed Mossadeq. The new Premier's first act on seizing power was systematically to undermine the 'corrupt and decadent' Shah and his 'worthless' young wife.

He had the support of both the military and the people, and, by plunging the country into a bitter international dispute with Britain over Persian oil, he weakened the position of its ruler. By refusing to fulfil export orders he brought the nation to the brink of financial and economic disaster. For a time it

seemed as if the Shah would be dethroned, and the danger to himself and Soraya grew so great that, in August 1953, they fled for safety to Rome.

There they listened to radio reports of rioting and looting in Teheran and to hysterical speeches demanding the execution of the Shah and his entire family. Soon, however, the royalist faction fought back and on August 19—after days of bloody street fighting—Mossadeq was himself overthrown and the Shah returned to the capital and the now joyful embrace of his people.

So far, Soraya's time as Empress had been even more arduous than her husband had predicted. The 30 months of the Mossadeq regime hardly came under the title, 'living happily ever afterwards', and the Shah determined to make up for this. By now they were genuinely in love with each other. From being married strangers they had grown to become adoring mates and friends. "Whatever it started out as," said one of their retinue, "there was no doubt about the marriage's new state. It was a love match."

To celebrate this—and to show his wife 12 years his junior that he could be full of sport and fun—the Shah decided they should put aside affairs of state for a time. While she admired and valued his qualities of courage and kindness, he came to rely upon her strength of character and commonsense. But enough was enough, he told her, from now on they were going to enjoy themselves!

So, in the winter of 1953, they entered a social, bubble world that they had previously tended to scorn and ignore. For almost the first time in their married life there were balls, parties, fancy dress parades, and reckless, windswept days as the Shah raced his 120 mph Mercedes across the desert. It was the kind of public life expected of modern royalty and it won them countless new admirers in other lands.

They were bombarded with requests to make state visits and, late in 1954, they embarked on the first of these. They went with pomp and splendor to England, to Germany—where, to Soraya's amusement, her hairdresser put her severed locks up for sale—to Iraq, and, in December, to the United States.

During this period of second-honeymoon it was expected that, finally after months of hope and prayer, Soraya would announce that she was with child. It didn't necessarily have to be a boy to start with, a girl would be all right as a first baby. After all, she was still only 22 years old and had years ahead of her in which to become the mother of three children, or maybe four.

"Motherhood was the one factor missing in her life," said a lady-in-waiting at the time. "Soraya had everything else she, or anyone else, could possibly wish for. A rich, handsome and devoted husband. Subjects who loved and respected her. All the clothes and jewels she could possibly need. But there was this gap, this absence, which grew bigger and bigger as the months passed. If maternal desire had anything to do with it, then she would have given birth there and then—to a boy!"

It was then, while in New York, that Soraya had the medical check which seemed to indicate that her sterility—if it had ever existed—was at an end. While in exile in Switzerland, three years later, awaiting the decision of the Wise Men, she thought wistfully of those happier days. "If only," she told a friend, "I could life my life over again I would change just one thing. I would have become pregnant a month after my wedding and would have had my first son before that year was out. By now, I would be the mother of at least three fine boys."

The Wise Men

But wishful thinking, however sincere, was of no help to her. Only the Wise Men could end her agony of suspense, let her know if she was to continue as the wife of the man she loved, or not. At the end of her fourth week in St Moritz it was announced that, almost 2000 miles away in Teheran, the decision about her own—and her country's—future had been made. But it would not be made public until Soraya was told the news in person.

This bleak announcement, and the fact that the Shah didn't jubilantly telephone her, made her fear for the worst. However, she was an Empress and must

The Shah with his son—the heir that Soraya could never produce—and his new Empress. On the day of their wedding, the old Empress spends a lonely day in Saint Moritz.

Popperfoto

63

behave like one. In the second week of March 1958, she prepared to meet the three emissaries sent specially from Persia to see her. They were ushered into her presence and it took only a brief glance at their sad faces and downcast eyes to realize the answer was: No.

"She listened to what they had to say in a kind of trance," said a friend afterwards. "The words themselves seemed to have no meaning for her. She just sat there and occasionally nodded her head. There was no point in trying to console or comfort her. I think she had known from the beginning what the answer would be, and had unconsciously steeled herself for it. When it was over she said simply, 'It's fate.'"

Stoicism

The Shah accepted the verdict with equal stoicism—and then acted with speed. The following day—March 15—he gave a brief statement to the effect that his marriage to Soraya had come to an end. There were difficulties of providing him with an heir which could not be solved. They were to be divorced.

With that there was nothing more to be said, and very little to be done. Soraya's clothes and belongings were sent to her parents' home in Cologne. She was diplomatically requested—if not ordered—not to set foot in her native Persia again. For her, divorce meant more than just a breaking of the marriage bond. It meant a rootless, footloose existence that was to take her on the high society and nightclub circuit, and from one companion to the next.

Before she started this pattern, however, she had to deal with a third and perhaps even more cruel blow. Eighteen months after her divorce was announced, her ex-husband married for the third time. His new bride was a statuesque Persian beauty, Farah Diba, who bore a noticeable physical resemblance to Soraya. "It wasn't a question of him marrying a particular type," said an observer at the time. "It was more as if he'd married Soraya all over again!"

However, it was a case of third time lucky for the Shah. Not only did he find affection and contentedness with the Empress Farah Diba, he also received the heir his royal position demanded. Within a year, his new wife gave birth to a fine healthy boy and the dynasty—in whose cause there had been so much suffering—was secured. But for Soraya, who was not to marry again, there was no such conveniently happy ending.

She was soon seen in restaurants and nightspots along the French and Italian Rivieras—and in capitals from Paris, to Monte Carlo, to Rome—on the arms of a squire of young men . . . most of whom were younger than herself, and none of whom resembled the Shah. And her

Tragedy followed Soraya wherever she went: rumors of her forthcoming marriage to Franco Indovina (top) were silenced when he died in a crash in 1972, and since she has had a succession of young companions.

romances were punctuated with rows, partings, and—in two cases—tragedy.

In 1972, for example, she seemed set to marry the handsome and talented Italian film director, Franco Indovina . . . who was killed in a plane crash that year. In 1975, at the mature age of 42—but as beautiful and desirable as ever—she was seen in Rome with 20-year-old student Francesco Napolitano. Later that year Napolitano had been changed for Texas oil heir Gerald Berheim. And yet another beau, French playboy Claude Kaouza, had died of a heart attack at the age of 28.

Then, in between unconfirmed rumors that she and the Shah had met clandestinely in Paris, and that she had become

desperately unhappy, a more permanent contender arrived in her life. The Naples industrialist Massimo Garcia, eight years her junior, had been photographed with her since 1974. And two years later he was still her escort.

That year, 1976, would have been the 25th anniversary of her marriage to the Shah. To mark what would have been a silver occasion, he sent her a gold, ruby-encrusted necklace. Heartened by this, she began to talk of returning to Persia as a tourist, and having a brief friendly meeting with the Shah. But the spring passed without the visit taking place.

Whatever may happen next in her unhappy, nomadic life, there is one thing that is certain. She will still reserve at least a part of her affections for her former husband. "In a sense," said a friend recently, "she is still married to the Shah. He was the first man in her life and, by rights, should have been the last. If she should ever marry again it will be a case of second-best."

BY H-BOMB TO THE STARS

As mankind reaches for the stars, one great obstacle stands in the way—power. Even the most massive modern missile would take far too long to accomplish useful interstellar flight. But one group of scientists claim they have found the clue to 'starflight' within a human lifetime . . . by harnessing the most ferocious power the world has known.

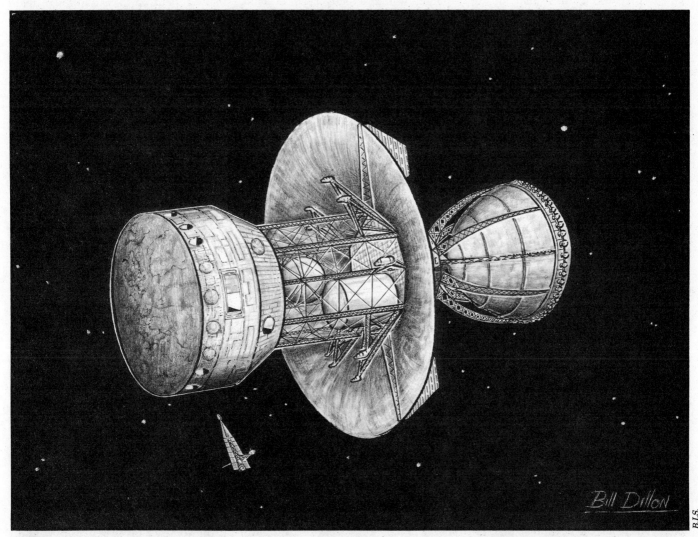

Bill Dillon

B.I.S.

The time is 50 years from now. High above the Earth, a small rocket's jets flare to push a steel-skeletoned spacecraft towards the outer reaches of the solar system. Suspended in the exosphere, the craft takes on fuel processed from the atmosphere of the giant planet Jupiter. Then, with a space-shattering roar, the craft lights up its fusion drive and blasts away from the solar system for ever . . . the first starship to cross the gulf to another sun.

It sounds like the imaginings of a science-fiction writer, or the beginning of a new television *Startrek* series. But it is, in fact, the clear-eyed prediction of an 11-man team of British astronomers and rocket engineers who are designing a craft to do what many experts have declared impossible. To reach the stars

A prototype of the H-bomb-propelled 'starship', developed by Alan Bond of the Blue Streak design team.

within a human lifetime. If their plans —code named Project Daedalus—work, the last great barrier to interstellar exploration could be swept away.

Already, the scientists have pinpointed their 'target star', 35-million-

million miles away. It is Barnard's Star, the second closest star to our own Sun, but too small and faint to be seen without a telescope. Even light, which crosses the space from the Earth to the Moon in just over a second, needs nearly six years to span the yawning gulf to Barnard's Star. The planned robot probe, speeding at its flat-out rate of 86 million miles-an-hour, would take 49.2 years.

The astronomers on the project chose Barnard's Star because it is believed to harbor the nearest planetary system in space to our own. The nearest star of all, Alpha Centauri, is less interesting because it is not thought to have planets.

From photographs taken of Barnard's Star over many years, scientists have found slight changes in its position which they think are due to the unbalancing effects of one or two orbiting planets. These planets are probably like the gas-covered giants of our solar system, Jupiter and Saturn.

Into the Unknown

But there may also be some smaller, unseen bodies like the Earth. And on one of those bodies, strange plants may flower or exotic animals squirm. Planetary systems may also exist round some of the other stars within a dozen or so light years of the Sun. Starships might eventually investigate these too.

The problem is *power*. Rocket power available today would certainly allow us to reach the stars; the hurdle is the immensely long time it would take. Even if we were content to just send an instrumented probe to the stars, the snag of that yawning transit-time remains until we can find a means of going much faster than is possible with the chemically-fuelled rockets of today.

And so the race to establish 'Power Power' is on. American and Soviet space engineers have already experimented with electric rockets, in which a stream of electrons is ejected in a fast-moving jet behind the craft. Unfortunately, the thrust of such a rocket is very low, and it would take a long time to push a large spacecraft up to high speed.

Perhaps the ultimate idea of all is the photon rocket, which would use particles of light called photons to generate thrust. The technical problems associated with building such a rocket are too fantastic to be even considered today; but it *has* the advantage that the speed of its exhaust is the highest that physics allows—the speed of light.

A charming variant on this idea proposes using the force of light from the Sun to waft a sail-powered craft round the sky, a sort of cosmic *Mayflower*. The pressure of sunlight is small, but it is enough to make the tails of comets flow so grandly. And solar energy is both free and endless.

Taking the brainwave a stage further, engineers have proposed using lasers, which are powerful emitters of light, to thrust into space a strong beam of radiation along which our *Mayflower* could ride.

Still more exotic is the proposal to use the thinly-spread gas between the stars as a fuel supply, scooped in by a massive magnetic saucer around the craft and fed into its reactor where nuclear power is released. The 'flying saucer' lives!

Such a craft, it has been calculated, could reach speeds quite close to that of light. It could also travel at an acceleration of 1g, which means that the occupants would feel as if they were under normal Earth gravity. Unlike traditional types of rocket, this craft, called a 'ramjet,' would actually perform at its best on the longest journeys, with more inter-stellar gas to scoop up.

If it is ever possible to build such a vessel—and the technology is certainly far beyond our present capabilities—the Universe would begin to open up to us. A manned ramjet could travel round the Milky Way, or even visit the Andromeda spiral galaxy, inside the lifetime of its crew; provided, of course, that we solve the physical problems of traveling close to the speed of light. Astronauts who rocket into space come back to Earth only fractions of a second younger than the rest of us. But for astronauts in a near-the-speed-of-light starship, weeks in space might equal centuries on Earth.

But this is gazing far into the future. More immediately, we can look forward to atomic-powered rockets which might be perfected for flight to the stars.

An atomic-powered rocket uses an atom-splitting reactor like those in nuclear submarines to generate heat. The heat can be used to expel a propellant in a high-speed jet. Or, in a miniaturized version of an atomic power station, it could generate electrical power so that it works like an electric rocket.

Perhaps a hybrid atomic-electric rocket would be the best compromise. And it is within reach of current technology—if we are willing to spend money on it. But its flight time to the nearest star would still be measured in centuries. And fully assembled it would weigh as much as several Saturn 5s.

No-one needs telling that there is a more explosive way of releasing nuclear energy than in a reactor. Literally 'bombing into space' is the only way we have at present of utilizing the energy of hydrogen fusion, the process thát powers the Sun. In a hydrogen bomb, light atoms are crushed together to make heavier substances. This actually releases more energy than the Hiroshima-type bomb, in which a very heavy atom is split into smaller parts.

It was this process which inspired the controversial new 'Daedalus Project.'

Surveying the possible propulsion mechanisms for a starship, rocket engineer Alan Bond—a former member of the Rolls-Royce 'Blue Streak' missile team and now with the British Aircraft Corporation at Stevenage, England —realized a staggering fact: that nuclear-bomb power presents us with a method of reaching the stars inside a human lifetime with the technology that is likely to be available by the year 2000. This clashes with the views of many experts who insist that high-speed interstellar travel will remain beyond our technical capacity for a very long time, if not for ever.

Project Daedalus

Bond went on to lead a design team that has outlined how such a mission might be accomplished. They worked under the name Project Daedalus, after the legendary Greek flier whose name means 'skillfully made'. The Daedalus team were backed by the British Interplanetary Society, which as long ago as the 1930s designed a Moonship that looked remarkably like the eventual Apollo lunar module.

The design now being sketched out by Bond, which has excited many space engineers in the United States, visualized the ship in two stages with an overall length of over 250 yards—about twice the size of the Moon-reaching Saturn 5. The vehicle, wherever it lights up from in the solar system, will be under boost for about 3.8 years—two years for the first stage and 1.8 years for the second. Then the engine switches off and the probe coasts towards Barnard's Star at its top speed of about 86 million miles-an-hour, 12.8 percent of the speed of light.

Total time for the flight is 49.2 years. Initially, the team were hoping for a shorter flight of about 40 years so that, should such a mission ever be mounted, it would be completed within the lifetimes of the youngest members of Mission Control. But they found that a slight increase in flight time meant they could more than halve the amount of propellant it would need to carry.

Detailed outline of the Daedalus starship, showing, at the top, the travelers' quarters, protected from radiation by a layer of graphite, and the bay which will house the space probe vehicles. Below it is the second stage reactor fed from huge round reservoirs of hydrogen which can be discarded when empty. At the bottom is the reaction chamber, supplied with 250 H-bombs per second through a magnetic injector. Compare the size of the starship to a scale outline of the Saturn 5.

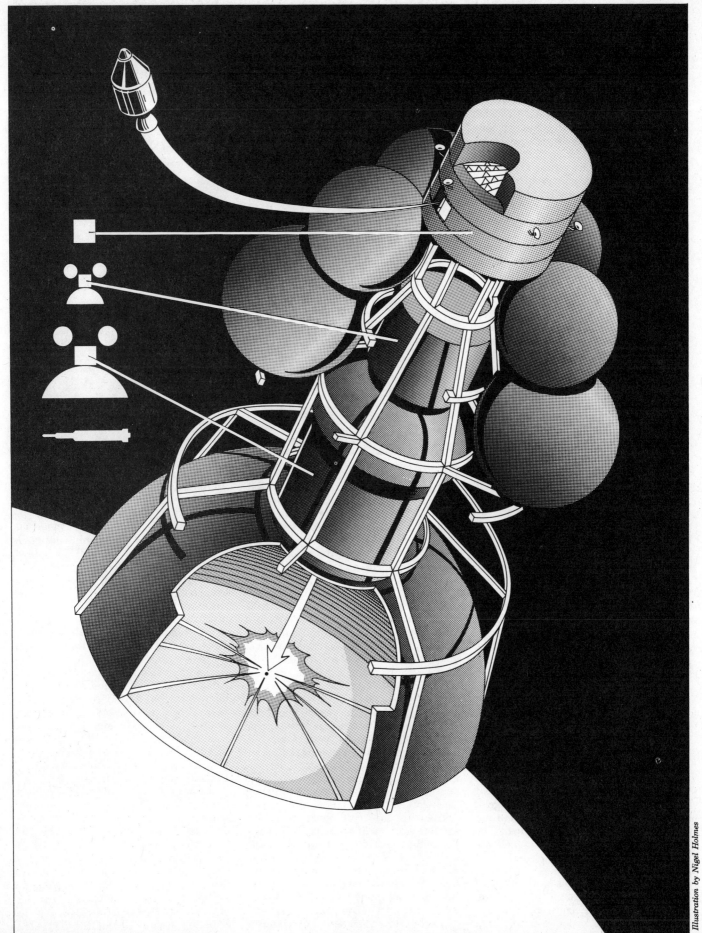

Illustration by Nigel Holmes

The Daedalus team decided on a starship with an overall weight of around 53 200 tons, carrying a payload of more than 450 tons—equal to six of America's Skylab space stations, currently the largest objects ever launched.

The massive payload is needed because the starship is designed to carry 20 smaller sub-probes, three of which will fly away from the mother ship during the coast period and radio back information on conditions between the stars. When Barnard's Star is reached, the remaining group of probes will set out to investigate the individual planets.

All this requires total on-board control by a central computer. "Because of the communication lag, once the probe is out near Barnard's Star, a two-way conversation takes 12 years," says Bond. "Therefore you cannot rely on instruction from Earth."

But the most daring and spectacular part of the craft is the propulsion system: Mini H-bombs are detonated behind the craft at a rate of 250 each second, and the energy of their blasts pushes the starship along.

Each bomb, which measures about half the size of a table-tennis ball, is a honeycomb structure made of deuterium and helium-3. But helium-3 is almost non-existent on Earth. It would have to be bred in special reactors on the Moon, or, in a more picturesque alternative, it could be sifted from the gases in the atmosphere of Jupiter where there is enough helium-3 to fuel 10 000 million such vehicles.

The starship team are planning very much for the next generation rather than themselves, because even once the technology becomes available it would still take about 20 years to build one such vessel. "The actual construction of the ship will probably take place in Moon orbit," says Bond. "It could then sail under auxiliary power to Jupiter to fuel up. The bombs will be made and loaded before the ship leaves on its voyage of discovery."

Bomb Power

The materials of the starship will mostly be titanium alloys and stainless steel, with aluminum alloys for the low-temperature fuel tanks. The reaction chamber in which the explosions actually occur, will be made of molybdenum to resist the enormous amounts of heat generated. A 40-ton beryllium screen protects the snub-nosed vehicle from impacts with particles in space. "The only exotic materials are the propellants themselves," says Bond.

The bombs, stored in their multi-millions in the first stage's six spherical fuel tanks, rattle through the starship's plumbing to the injector, which uses a magnetic gun to shoot them at high

speed into the center of the reaction chamber. "The bomb rides down a constriction in the magnetic field," explains Bond. "It's a bit like swallowing."

In the center of the combustion chamber, the bomb is hit by energetic beams from electron guns spaced round the chamber's rim and it ignites with an explosive force equal to more than 90 tons of TNT. Inside the chamber is a magnetic field which absorbs the blast, and pushes the probe along like a kind of magnetic spring. In a few millionths of a second the effects of the blast are over and the chamber is ready to receive the next bomb. If a bomb fails to ignite, it has no real effect on the starship's final velocity.

Once top speed is reached and the starship begins to coast, its combustion chamber can be used as a giant communications dish to radio back data on conditions in space. Two automated pods may fly around the craft to effect repairs and position or monitor experimental 'packages.'

Then, as the craft nears its target, smaller probes will be dispatched to give the widest possible picture of another solar system in space—information that will help to put our own planetary system into perspective and maybe answer that nagging question, 'Are we alone?'

What can the controllers on Earth expect to learn as the radio signals

One possible source of power for space travel might be solar energy, caught, like the wind, in 'sails'.

complete their six-year travel time from Barnard's Star? The starship's designers are confident that we will be able to receive TV pictures from Barnard's Star. There may be as many as 4000 photographs to be relayed back to Earth after the encounter, at a rate of one every few hours.

The team's communications expert, Tony Lawton, envisages that the sub-probes would relay their information via the mother ship. "We may actually see surface features on some of the larger planets surrounding Barnard's Star," he says. It will be like staring at Earth's 'double' . . . but as for signs of life? These would be too small to notice. Analysis of satellite pictures of the Earth shows that very fine detail is needed before signs of life show up.

The way to answer that question with finality would be to mount a manned mission . . . with the risk of sentencing astronauts to an eternity in space. But by then, scientists are convinced, mankind will already be firmly established on a 'halfway house' in space; a vast floating colony where thousands, maybe millions, of people will be born, live and die without ever even setting foot on Mother Earth.

VOICES FROM THE DEAD

Under hypnosis, the character of the Colorado housewife slowly changed. She was getting younger. Then, to the amazement of the listeners, she began describing her previous life—and death—as Bridey Murphy, in 19th-century Ireland. Was this at last the proof that believers in reincarnation had been hoping for . . . or just the beginning of an elaborate hoax?

Popperfoto

One cold November night in 1952 three sober, adult, middle-class Americans heard a little girl's voice issue from the hypnotized body of a 29-year-old woman. "My name is Bridey . . . Bridey Murphy . . . I live in Ireland . . . I am eight years old . . . the year is 1806."

It was the start of a bizarre hunt for the identity of the 'voice' and the beginning of a controversy which was to shake psychical research circles for a decade. For in conducting the curious experiment which produced such startling results, the hypnotist, Morey Bernstein, had set out to prove that reincarnation—the center of belief to millions of the world's Buddhists and Hindus—is, literally, a fact of life.

Bernstein was an unlikely figure to have ventured upon such an undertaking. A tough Westerner in his early thirties, he was a graduate of the University of Pennsylvania's Wharton School of Finance, and sales director of his family firm, Bernstein Brothers Equipment, of Pueblo, Colorado. The company sold hardware to the ranchers and farmers of the State, everything from tractors to cattle prods, baling wire to half-inch screws, and when he was not punching the virtues of his products home to his hard-bitten clientele, Bernstein spent his time socializing. He read nothing but novels and business magazines, and, unlike his pretty wife Hazel, he knew of and cared nothing for 'occult stuff'.

Then, some three years before the appearance of 'Bridey Murphy,' Morey Bernstein went to a cocktail party and watched an amateur hypnotist inveigle a girl into taking off one of her shoes and stockings. He was unimpressed by the simple show. He asked the hypnotist for some proof that the girl really was under his power, that she was not in collaboration with him, that the whole thing was not a spoof.

At the end of the evening Bernstein returned home baffled. He was still cynical, but he was fair: he could offer no explanation as to what had occurred in the practical terms he knew and trusted, so he sent off to a mail order publisher for half a dozen books dealing with hypnosis.

"When the books came," he said, "I stopped reading novels. Even magazines and trade journals were neglected to some extent. I just couldn't tear myself away from the hypnotism books; I was utterly enchanted. I was . . . overwhelmed by a single question: Why hasn't science done more with this near miracle?"

For the next few years Bernstein studied his newfound subject, teaching himself to hypnotize almost anyone with comparative ease. Soon he was helping

neighbors and friends to overcome minor ailments by means of his skill; he cured his wife of persistent headaches, rid a friend's nephew of a lifelong stammer, and successfully treated others for migraine, insomnia, and excessive smoking. Despite his lack of 'official' qualification, the medical profession seems to have aided and encouraged him, and on more than one occasion he helped a local doctor treat patients with psychosomatic problems.

To do this, he used the technique of 'age regression.' The theory behind the technique was simple enough; somewhere along the subject's life-line there was a knot, perhaps a psychological snarl-up caused by some simple childhood happening, which had lasting repercussions in the subject's adult life. To untie this knot the subject was put into deep trance and then 'conducted' back over the years, until the time of the original conflict was reached. The hypnotist then told the patient that all was well, pointing out the origin of the difficulty and soothing away the anxiety. And in a striking number of cases it worked—and still does.

Back to Infancy

The physical effect on the subject was fascinating. The voice of a grown man would often 'lighten' into that of a prepubertal child, and become regressively childlike in its vocabulary, and a subject told to write his name while at, say, the 'hypnotic' age of six, would do so in the manner of a six-year-old.

An especially convincing proof of the veracity of 'hypnotic age' was confirmed by Leslie Le Cron, an early experimental hypnotist, who showed that tickling of the sole of the foot of an adult under hypnosis caused the big toe to turn downward—a process known as flexion. In infants up to about seven months of age, however, the toes turn upward —dorsiflexion—and this was exactly what happened to the feet of adults 'regressed' to a similar age by hypnosis.

It was the technique of 'age regression' which set Bernstein on the track of the mysterious Bridey Murphy phenomenon. If a person could be taken back in a trance state to the period of his earliest infancy, why not attempt to take him back to the womb—and whatever lay beyond?

This final train of thinking was set in motion, however, by a good deal of preliminary speculation on Bernstein's part. His discovery of the powers of hypnosis seems to have awakened a dormant interest in the powers of the mind in general; when members of his family experienced examples of what appeared to be telepathy and precognitive dreams, he and a colleague, Bill Meery, began experimenting with the

ability of subjects to 'mind read' while under hypnosis. They had only a limited amount of success, but it was sufficient to interest Dr. Joseph Banks Rhine, head of the famous parapsychology unit at Duke University, North Carolina.

While delving further into the paranormal, Morey Bernstein came upon a book dealing with the extraordinary American 'health reader' Edgar Cayce, who had died in 1945, some years before. Cayce, a Kentucky farmboy born in 1877, had had an uncanny ability to diagnose first his own, then other people's illnesses while in hypnotic trance. Although he had little or no formal schooling, Cayce used complicated medical terms while diagnosing, setting out exactly what was wrong in each case, and what should be done

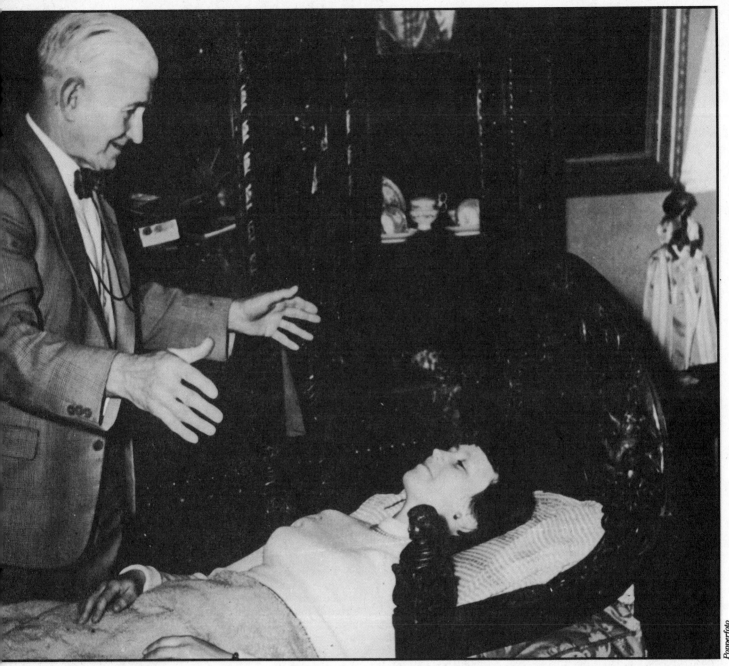

about the condition. Many doctors became interested in him, and out of an estimated 30 000 'readings', one eminent medical man from Delaware, who had studied them all, claimed a diagnostic accuracy of over 90 percent for Cayce and his puzzling talents.

But the aspect of Cayce's clairvoyant gifts which intrigued Bernstein most was his so called 'life readings.' The Kentucky seer had, apparently, accurately forecast the progress of about 2500 men and women in the manner of an astrologer reading a birth chart, with the major difference that he claimed to see their past 'lives' on earth and used these as a basis for his forecasts.

Bernstein at first scorned the idea of reincarnation and then, as with hypnosis and parapsychology, decided to dig

further. He discovered that, to believers, reincarnation was a form of evolution. As Dr. Gina Cerminara puts it in her book on Edgar Cayce, *Many Mansions*: "The soul is like an actor who takes different roles and wears different costumes on different nights."

He discovered too that many great intellects had accepted reincarnation, among them Schopenhauer, Emerson, Walt Whitman, Goethe, Pythagoras and Plato. And at this point Bernstein made up his mind; he would try the age regression process on a subject picked at random, and push it to its ultimate limit.

A suitable subject sprang readily to mind. She was known by the name 'Ruth Mills Simmons'—her real identity was not revealed till many years later—and she was the wife of a successful sales-

With a candle in his hand, Morey Bernstein hypnotizes his best subject, Ruth Simmons, and records her transition beyond death into 'Bridey Murphy'.

man named Rex who looked, according to Hazel Bernstein, exactly like Tyrone Power. Ruth herself was a pretty and vivacious brunette of 29 whose native state was Iowa, but who had lived in Colorado since her teens. She and her handsome husband were highly popular at parties, and it was at one of these that the Bernsteins had met the couple. Fascinated by Bernstein's reputation as a hypnotist, Ruth had begged him to 'put her under' and he had discovered to his delight that she was a near perfect hypnotic subject. On several occasions since he had 'regressed' her to the age of one year, and her memories had been astonishingly clear and convincing. When he told her of his plan to take regression to the ultimate stage and asked her to take part, Ruth willingly agreed.

On Saturday, November 29, 1952, a cold clear evening, Rex and Ruth Simmons arrived at Bernstein's home, where he and his wife Hazel were waiting. The time was 10.30 p.m., and after only a short preliminary chat Bernstein set his tape recorder rolling and, five minutes later, began the process of putting Ruth into a trance. After a slow count of three, during which she stared into a candle flame as Morey Bernstein droned soothingly to her, Ruth's head fell sideways onto the cushion of the sofa where she was lying, and her breathing became deep and regular.

"We are going to turn back through time and space, just like turning the pages of a book. And when I next talk to you . . . when I next talk to you . . . you will be seven years old . . ."

Beyond the Grave

The session was successful so far. In a high, childlike voice Ruth Simmons recounted details of her school and her classmates. On Bernstein's gentle instructions she slid back a further two years, talking of her favorite game, hopscotch, her dolls, and her little dog Buster. Further and further they slipped, past memories stored deep past the reach of the conscious mind, until Ruth reached one year old. She babbled like a baby. Bernstein leaned towards her.

"Back, back, and back . . . until oddly enough you find yourself in some other scene, some other place, some other time, and when I talk to you again you will tell us about it."

For long moments the room was in absolute silence, apart from the faint whirring of the tape recorder and Ruth's heavy breathing. Then her lips stirred, and another childlike voice, this time with an unfamiliar accent, said '. . . scratched the paint off all my bed!'

Bernstein didn't understand. He hesitated, and then asked the only question logical under the circumstances: "Why did you do that?"

Soft and relaxed, the 'new voice' told how 'she' had been spanked and sent to bed for some childish offence, and had taken revenge on a grown-up world by picking the paint off her freshly painted metal bed. When she grew silent again, Bernstein asked: "What is your name?"

And Ruth Mills Simmons answered: "Friday . . . Friday Murphy."

All three listeners swore later that the name had first appeared as 'Friday,' although they were soon to be corrected.

For the next few hours the three

observers listened with growing astonishment as Bernstein calmly probed the 'memory' of this new entity. Her real name was Bridey Murphy, she lived in Cork, Ireland, with her father, a lawyer named Duncan, and her mother Kathleen. She had a brother, also named Duncan, and they lived together in a white, wooden house. She was eight and the year was 1806.

Her hair was, she said, 'real red'—as distinct from the brunette of Ruth's own coloring—and she went to Mrs Strayne's Day School. She ate milk and fruit for breakfast. Carefully, Bernstein took her 'forward' through her life, at each stage questioning her for details. She had married a Belfast lawyer named Brian MacCarthy, a Catholic—she herself was a Protestant—and had gone to live with him in the north. They went to church at St. Theresa's, where the priest was Father John. They had no children. At Bernstein's insistence she pronounced a few 'typical' Irish words—'banshee' 'colleen' and 'brate', which was, she said, a kind of drinking cup.

And then she came to the most dramatic moment of all: her 'death' and what lay after. Bridey Murphy, it transpired, had died at the age of sixty-six, after falling downstairs.

Death's Secrets

"Can you tell us what happened after your death? Can you tell us what happened after you died?"

"I didn't do . . . like Father John said. I didn't go to purgatory. I stayed right in that house until Father John died. Oh he died . . . I saw him. I saw him when he died."

"And then you talked to him?"

"Yes."

With an atavistic chill he could hardly suppress, Bernstein realized that he might well be questioning a ghost. For the 'spirit' of Bridey Murphy told how she had watched her husband die—although she had not been able to speak to his 'spirit' and had then returned to Cork, where she had tried to speak to her brother Duncan, still living in old age.

"He couldn't see me."

Vaguely, the 'ghost' remembered wandering—feeling neither emotion nor desire—for 'a long time.' Then she was reborn again in Iowa, as Ruth Mills. There the session ended, after corroborative questions from the hypnotist.

Between that first night and October 1953 Morey Bernstein conducted six more trance interviews with the voice of Bridey Murphy. Hundreds of tiny details were added to the first basic outline of her life and death, some clear, some hazy. Perhaps the most fascinating result of all came during the third session, when 'Bridey' said she could dance an Irish jig. Bernstein told her that,

after she awoke again as Ruth Simmons, she would perform the dance for the observers. Sure enough Ruth, who claimed never to have danced a jig before, performed a jig with flying, nimble feet and dainty steps.

For the next two years, Bernstein's new obsession—the conviction that he had 'proved' the theory of reincarnation as far as was possible—impinged on his hectic business life. He took the tapes with him to New York, and played them to after-dinner audiences of doctors, lawyers and other professional men, some of whom were skeptical, others less so. Finally a representative of Hutchinson, the publishing company, suggested he write a book on the subject. But first he should try to establish whether or not any tangible proof existed of Bridey

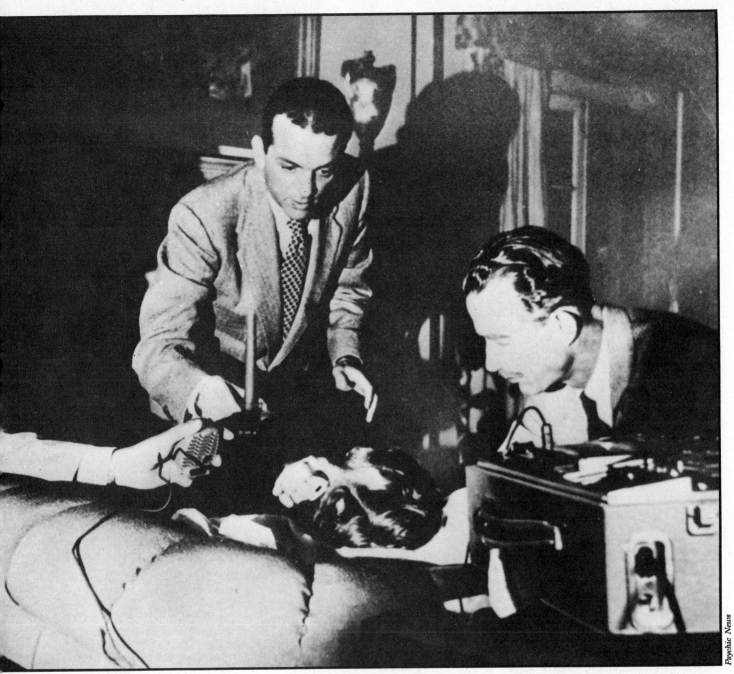

Murphy's 'real' life in Ireland.

To keep the investigation as objective as possible, the publishers appointed an Irish legal firm, various librarians, and a team of professional researchers to carry it out, without revealing their names to Morey Bernstein. But Murphy was one of the most frequent surnames in Ireland, and perhaps predictably, the lengthy search was disappointing.

One or two facts uncovered were, however, of interest. An Irish lawyer reported that a John McCarthy, a Roman Catholic from Cork, had appeared on the registers of King's Inn, Cork in 1830. 'Bridey' had said that her father-in-law, a Catholic lawyer had practiced in Cork—although she spelled his name 'MacCarthy.'

She also reported that while in Belfast

she had bought 'foodstuffs' at shops owned by a Mr Farr and a Mr Carrigan. A Belfast librarian confirmed that shops of both names had existed at the relevant time. These three facts were, unfortunately, as far as anything like 'solid' evidence went. Bridey had mentioned various places, most of which could be found in any modern atlas. The Irish words she used—'banshee' and 'colleen'—were hardly esoteric, even to a Colorado housewife, while her favorite song, *The Londonderry Air* was equally well known. Belfast had a church called St. Theresa's, but there were many hundreds of the same name in Ireland.

Nevertheless, when Bernstein published his book *The Search for Bridey Murphy* in 1955 it entered the bestseller lists and caused enormous newspaper

Bernstein's technique of taking his subjects back to a previous incarnation has been expanded by Arnall Bloxham, the Welsh hypnotist.

speculation. It was later made into a 'supernatural' movie. Although Ruth Simmons herself showed little interest in the subject after the first flush of publicity, Bernstein made lecture tours and appeared on television.

And then the bubble burst when a newspaperman discovered that Mrs Simmons, who had been orphaned early in her life, had been raised by a Norwegian uncle and an aunt of Scottish and Irish extraction. There, surely, lay the answer. Tales from her distant childhood, of Irish history and customs, had lodged

A.P.

themselves in Ruth Simmons' subconscious, only to re-emerge under hypnosis as the experiences of Bridey Murphy.

Or had they? Even the most rigorous investigators failed to catch either Bernstein or Mrs Simmons out in anything smacking of conscious fraud. The only logical explanation seemed to be that she was suffering from cryptoamnesia—the conscious 'forgetting' of thousands of tiny details read or seen on film, or otherwise amassed during an ordinary lifetime. As, sometimes, such forgotten facts re-emerge in dreams, so hypnosis had brought them out.

But not everyone believed this. In Cardiff, Wales, for instance, a hypnotherapist named Arnall Bloxham and his wife Dulcie decided to take the same road as that trodden by Morey and Hazel Bernstein. To date, Mr and Mrs Bloxham have over 400 hours of taped interviews by subjects who have been 'regressed' as Ruth Simmons was. The tapes cover records of 'lives' in every social class and every period of history, and although many are as humdrum as the Bridey Murphy story, one or two

appear to throw light on history.

Perhaps the most dramatic of Bloxham's tapes was that recorded by a woman who claimed to have been Henriette, exiled sister of Charles II of England. The sitter, who had no specialized knowledge of the Stuart period, nevertheless was able to give a remarkable account of the court of Louis XIV of France, of his brother Philippe, Duc D'Orléans, to whom Henriette was married, of 'La Grande Mademoiselle' Duchess of Montpensier, of Prince Rupert of Palatine, and of many other notable figures of the time. Speaking of her 'father', Charles I, the sitter says sadly, "Papa was killed in London . . . they murdered him."

Mrs Dulcie Bloxham, who researches details given under hypnosis, sums up the problems which face her and which faced Morey Bernstein. "If a tape is historically accurate, it is said that the sitter has reproduced recorded facts out of his subconscious, however obscure and however unlikely it seems that the sitter can have had access to the little known details. If, on the other hand, the

Bridey Murphy took a leap in time to reappear as 'Mrs Ruth Simmons' in the 20th century. But Ruth Simmons was itself a pseudonym to protect Morey Bernstein's subject from the press. Her real name was Mrs Tighe, and later she remarried to become Mrs Morrow. Tracked down by journalists she was asked: Had she ever tried to recapture Bridey again? She replied "It has been 20 years since I was Bridey Murphy. I have never done anything like it again and I never will."

tape does not give any facts which can be checked historically, then the charge is made that no known details are given. All the sincere researcher can do is to accumulate more and more 'lifes' in the hope that one day something irrefutable, something concrete, will come up."

So far, it seems, no such solid data has emerged to prove the existence or otherwise of previous lives on earth. So Bridey Murphy remains a matter for speculation . . . except to those who are already convinced.

I SURVIVED THE ROYAL MASSACRE

On July 16, 1918, the entire Russian royal family was murdered in a cellar by Red troops. Or were they? Two years later, the 'dead' Princess Anastasia reappeared in Germany. She said she had survived the shooting and been smuggled out of Russia. But not everyone believed her incredible story . . .

Popperfoto

John Frost

Popperfoto

The Berlin streets were frost-covered that night in February 1920, and Sergeant Hallman of the city police found his patrol duty discomfortingly quiet and uneventful. Stamping his feet and rubbing his hands, he wished something would happen to take his mind off the cold and the boredom. Then, as he approached the bridge over the Landwehr Canal, he saw the figure of a young woman poised on the parapet of the Bendler Bridge. She gazed down into the dark, slow-moving water. Suddenly, without uttering a sound, she threw herself into the river.

Pulling off his greatcoat, Sergeant Hallman ran forward and dived in after her. He grabbed hold of the would-be suicide and managed to drag her semi-conscious body ashore. She put up no resistance and the sergeant carried her back onto the bridge. A few minutes later an ambulance arrived and took the bedraggled girl to the Elizabeth Hospital. There it was found that she had no papers or identification documents, no valuables of any kind, and no money on her.

The next day, worried by the patient's seeming indifference to whether she lived or died, the doctors transferred her to Berlin's Dalldorf Psychiatric Hospital. There psychiatrists diagnosed that she was suffering from a deep and probably prolonged depression. Tests suggested that she had lost her memory and she was put in one of the non-violent wards.

Weeks went by and the girl—quite pretty with her long brown hair, chiseled nose and soulful eyes—remained like a vegetable. Then another of the inmates —a fat, middle-aged woman named Klara Peuthert—read an article in an illustrated magazine about the murder, two years previously, of the Czar of Russia and his family.

Thunderbolt

There were several pictures of Czar Nicholas II, his wife, Alexandra, his son and heir, Alexei, and his four attractive daughters—Anastasia, Tatiana, Maria and Olga. At first Fraülein Peuthert couldn't decide what it was about Anastasia—who was aged 16 when the photograph had been taken—that so puzzled and intrigued her. Then the answer came to her like 'a God-directed thunderbolt.'

The nameless girl in her ward and the girl in the picture could be twins. Admit-

tedly there was an age difference of some four or five years. But, if the teenage Princess Anastasia *had not* been shot by members of the Bolshevist Red Guard, she could have grown up to look exactly like the girl with no identity. Fraülein Peuthert hurriedly reported her theory to the hospital doctors. In turn, they contacted one of the dead Czarina's former ladies-in-waiting, Baroness Buxhoevan, who came to inspect the mystery girl. She took one look at her and declared, "There is no doubt about it. This child is the Czar's youngest daughter, the Princess Anastasia!"

A short while later, the girl now thought to be Anastasia found that her mental block had been lifted. Stating that, in fact, she *was* the supposedly dead princess (Anastasia had been born on January 5, 1901, in Peterhof Castle near St. Petersburg, then the capital of Russia and today called Leningrad), she told a story that was fantastic and yet plausible.

The Bolshevik revolution—which ended 300 years of rule by the Romanov family and gave power to the people —took place in November 1917. It was then that the Czar and his family were put under house arrest in the industrial town of Yekaterinburg (today Sverdlovsk). Their lives had been assured, but as the months passed there was talk of a royalist plot to rescue them. This convinced the leader of the Red Army, Lev Trotsky, that the royalists must be 'disposed of'. Orders were accordingly given for them to be shot without warning.

On July 16, 1918, Anastasia and her family went to bed as usual at around 10 o'clock. Then, in the middle of the night, they were abruptly awakened and told to dress. Anastasia put on some light shoes and a skirt into which a valuable pearl necklace and some emeralds had been sewn, and accompanied her family down to the cellar.

"When we got downstairs," she stated, "and were taken into a large room, I felt terrified. My sister Olga was the calmest. Papa carried Alexei. Mama was half fainting with fear and, being almost unconscious, she perhaps took in least of all the appalling things that were happening to us.

"As soon as we were all in the room, the soldiers began firing at us with revolvers . . . I can remember standing behind Olga, trying to hide behind her shoulder, and I know I saw Papa, her, and Alexei being hit. But I don't remember anything after that, I had lost consciousness."

On The Run

She knew nothing more until some hours later—when she came-to and found herself in a cart, traveling by night, and in the company of two strange soldiers. Although she didn't then know it, her father, mother, sisters and brother had been secretly buried outside Yekaterinburg at a disused mine called 'The Mine of the Four Brothers'—and she was the closest surviving relative of the Czar.

"My head ached dreadfully," she later wrote in her autobiography, *I, Anastasia*. "It was covered with wet cloths, and my hair was sticky with blood. I must have had a high fever. My only wish was that this terrible shaking, which was making my head burst, would stop.

"Now and then I must have cried out in pain and despair. I heard the voices of people I didn't know, who were looking after me without my being able to ask them. I could now feel that I was lying on straw, and I smelt the vinegar and onions they were rubbing me with to bring me round. Sometimes they lifted me out of the cart and carried me for part of the way so as to lessen my agony."

She had no idea how long the journey lasted—it may have been weeks, it may have been months. All she was aware of was the cold, the pain, and the constant fear of being recaptured.

Mansell

"I was traveling the woods and roads like the gypsies," she stated, "sick and unwashed, with the wretched feeling that something terrible had happened . . . When I look back on it even today, I am still overcome with an agony of terror. On the other hand, I can remember the indescribable sense of relief I felt on hearing from my rescuers that we had crossed the Rumanian frontier."

By then she had learnt from her companions that they were brothers, Alexander and Serge Tschaikovsky—members of the Red Guard who were nevertheless faithful to the Czar. Alexander was particularly sympathetic and he described how he and Serge had taken pity on her after the mass execution—in which she had somehow managed to avoid being struck by a bullet. They succeeded in sneaking her blanket-wrapped body onto a cart-like sledge instead of the lorry bound for the burial place.

From that moment on they had been on the run. Only now, as they entered the Rumanian capital, Bucharest, could they afford to relax and forget about the past. . . .

It seemed only natural, therefore, that

For months the Czar and his family were held in captivity by the Bolsheviks (above) until they were considered too much of a threat, and shot. In the press coverage of this event, a family portrait (left) reached the hospital where an unknown girl was being treated for amnesia: she bore an uncanny likeness to the young Princess Anastasia . . .

Alexander and Anastasia should become man and wife. Because of the 'nervous fever' which seldom left her, Anastasia stayed in the house they rented—only leaving it to be married. The baby she later gave birth to was delivered at home. Then, shortly after this, tragedy did catch up with the fugitive princess. Her husband was mysteriously shot dead in the street and she ventured outside for only the second time—to attend Alexander's funeral.

When the funeral was over, and her baby son had been placed in an orphanage, she had no reason to stay in Bucharest. She decided to move on to Germany, and her brother-in-law, Serge, agreed to go with her. On arriving in Berlin she sold the last of the jewels that had been stitched into her clothes and rented two rooms in a cheap hotel. Serge went out on an errand saying he would be back soon. Several hours later, however, he hadn't returned and Anastasia felt deserted.

She went outside to look for him and spent hours drifting vacantly through the cold city streets. Finally, almost too tired to walk any further, she came to the bridge over the canal and succumbed to "the pain in my head, my despair and my loneliness." The rest of her bizarre tale was known to the authorities, who now believed that they had the Princess, or Grand-Duchess, Anastasia of Russia in their care. And care was the thing she needed most in the world.

Depressive

She was still considered a 'depressive character,' and her mental and physical ailments (she suffered from bad teeth, poor eyesight, and the after-effects of strain and malnutrition) took her from one hospital and clinic to another. Altogether, she spent most of the next seven years in nursing homes or being looked after by newly-made friends.

According to Detective Inspector Grunberg, of the Berlin police, who made a special study of her case, Anastasia presented "an historical mystery comparable to that of the Man in the Iron Mask." He felt that her true identity would never be known, and was not entirely convinced by the medical evidence which suggested that she really was of Russian royal blood.

Doctors' examinations showed that Anastasia in her mid-twenties had the same physical characteristics as Anastasia as a teenager—bunions, especially on the right foot; a small white scar on the shoulder-blade from a cauterized mole; a scar on the forehead caused by a childhood fall; a scar on the middle finger of the left hand when it was caught in a coach door; and, the only addition, a scar behind the right ear possibly caused by a glancing bullet.

However, despite this 'proof,' many people felt that Anastasia was a fake. It was claimed that she couldn't speak a word of Russian—though some said she spoke it fluently in her sleep. The controversy about her spread throughout Europe. Then, in the summer of 1927, a private detective provided seemingly damning evidence against her.

He claimed that she was really a Polish peasant girl called Franziska Senanzkovsky, who had disappeared from her apartment in Berlin on February 15, 1920—three days before 'Anastasia' was pulled out of the canal. He also produced a statement by the daughter of Franziska's landlady that the Pole and the woman calling herself Anastasia were one and the same.

The 'pretender's' answer to this was twofold—a flat denial and an announcement that she was shortly leaving for the United States, where she would stay with her cousin Princess Xenia at her home at Oyster Bay, New York.

The Grand-Duchess Anastasia sailed for the New World the following February aboard the liner *Berengaria*. She hadn't seen Xenia (whose father, the Grand Duke Georgy Mihailovitch, had been shot in St. Petersburg in 1918) since they were children, and she longed for their reunion. Since fleeing to the US, Xenia had married a millionaire industrialist, William Leeds, and on February 28, 1928, Mr Leeds told a reporter from the New York *Daily News*: "It will probably never be proved whether the young lady at present staying with Mrs Leeds is or is not the Grand-Duchess. At any rate she herself will make no efforts to prove her identity to the Russian circles close to the Romanovs who doubt her genuineness. Her present chaperone, the former Princess Xenia of Russia, believes in her identity, and that is enough."

Three months later—after writing to relatives in Europe that Anastasia was the 'real thing'—Mrs Leeds said in an

Though she was known as 'Mrs Tchaikovsky' or 'Anna Anderson' in later years, 'Anastasia' never gave up her claim to the throne of Russia.

interview with the New York *World* that, "As a child I often played with Anastasia, who was the same age as I. Mrs Tchaikovsky (as Anastasia called herself in the United States) has astonished me by recalling where and what we played. She also reminded me of other events. I have not the slightest doubt as to her identity and am ready to stake all my money to prove it."

However, such a rash move wasn't necessary. In an attempt to have her identity established once and for all (and to be awarded the Czar's fortune of $10 million), Anastasia returned to Europe and began the first of the long legal suits that were to plague her for the next 30 or more years. One court case after another ended indecisively until—in 1967—a Hamburg court of appeal finally rejected both her claims.

By then, however, Anastasia—who had taken the name Anna Anderson in a desperate bid for privacy—had retired to a hut in Germany's Black Forest. But a year later, according to some European sources, she quietly married and went back to the United States. Disillusioned with the world, and in particular with lawyers, judges and journalists, she prepared to spend her last years away from the limelight . . . trying to forget the nightmare which started in November 1917, and which, for her, never seemed to end.

IT CAN'T BE TRUE... THEY'VE SHOT BOBBY!

With frightful malevolence, the Curse of the Kennedys seemed bent on annihilating the entire family. Tragedy had struck so many times, culminating in the shooting of President Kennedy. Now his brother lay dying from another assassin's bullets.

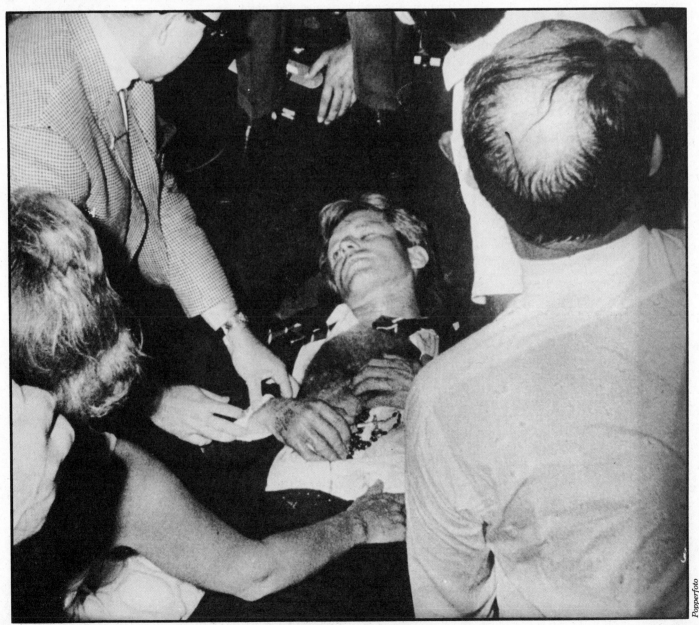

John F. Kennedy once said, "Just as I went into politics when Joe died, if anything happened to me tomorrow my brother Bobby would run for my seat. And if anything happened to him, my brother Teddy would run for us."

And so it happened that the Curse of the Kennedys was passed from brother to brother.

Joe Jr. was dead. John was dead. Now it was Bobby's turn to take up the reins of fate and the presidential challenge, to try to keep the name of Kennedy a living force in the political hierarchy of America.

But still the almost supernatural misfortune that had haunted the family for so many years continued. On June 19, 1964, just seven months after the assassination of President Kennedy in Dallas, tragedy struck yet again.

Once more the ill-fated clan were to gather together in grief. Once more courageous Rose Kennedy and her paralyzed husband Joe were to learn that another of their children was critically hurt. This time the victim was to be their youngest son, Edward.

Always the baby of the nine Kennedy children, Teddy was growing up. At 32 he was already a senator and better liked in the Senate than either of his big brothers. In fact, John had once admitted that Ted was "the best politician in the family." And George McGovern, South Dakota's Democratic senator, said of him, "He is more conservative and orthodox politically than Bob. In the broad sense, Ted has the greatest personal appeal of all the Kennedys."

On the evening of June 19, Teddy was still working. At 7.49 p.m. he voted in Washington for Bobby's hard-fought-for civil rights bill. Then, together with his close friend and aide, Ed Moss, and another young senator, Birch Bayh of Indiana, and Bayh's wife, Ted Kennedy took off from Washington National Airport in a private chartered plane to attend the Massachusetts Democratic State Convention at West Springfield.

Ted was to accept the convention's nomination as candidate for the full-term Senate seat once held by his brother. For two years Ted had filled the unexpired part of the term. Senator Bayh was to be the convention's key speaker.

As the pilot, Edwin Thomas Zimny, neared Barnes Airport in Westfield he asked for a weather report. Foggy, visibility poor. He prepared to land on Runway 20.

Suddenly, Senator Bayh noticed what he thought were black clouds out of the plane's left window. In fact they were the tops of 65-foot trees. Seconds later the plane tore into the trees and crashed into an apple orchard.

Zimny, the pilot, died instantly, crushed with the cockpit. The Bayhs managed to crawl through an 18-inch window pulling an unconscious Kennedy after them, the only person in the plane not to have fastened his seat belt.

A local farmer, Robert Sahuer, discovered the devastated plane and its injured passengers and went for help. Ted Kennedy insisted that the others go in the first ambulance and waited for the second one to take him to the emergency ward in nearby Northampton. He had fractured his spine in six places, broken two ribs and was covered with cuts and bruises. "It's amazing he is alive," one of the doctors marveled. Nonetheless, his condition was critical.

Ed Moss fought for his own life for seven hours and then died. And it seemed his friend Ted would follow him.

Bedridden

But the Kennedy stamina won through, although it seemed Ted might never walk again. A woman working in the hospital's coffee shop summed up the feelings of the world when she asked, "How much do these people have to give?" At least, on this occasion, it was not to be the life of yet another son.

For six months, Kennedy was bedridden, in traction for most of the time. Eventually he was able to progress to a wheel chair and then to crutches. He had to spend long periods retraining muscles, rebuilding his body. During his convalescence he carried on with important Senate work and read a great deal. He was determined that he would walk unaided into the Senate for the start of the second session of the 88th Congress in January 1965. He did. Fifteen pounds thinner, but alive.

He had been re-elected by an even bigger margin than two years previously, winning 1 716 907 votes to his opponent's 587 663.

Robert, too, was elected as senator to New York despite his earlier assurance that he did not intend to run. It was the first time in the history of the United States that one family had produced three senators. But it was an achievement the Kennedys were to pay for dearly over the years.

For still the curse continued, constantly piercing the glittering shell of the Kennedys and all who chose to share their lives.

In the case of Ethel, the soft-hearted wife of Bobby Kennedy, tragedy came again and again. First her parents were both killed in an Oklahoma air crash in 1955, then eleven years later her brother, George, was also killed in a private plane crash in Idaho along with Bobby's close friend Dean Markham. And then, just eight months later, her brother's widow was having dinner with her children when a piece of meat got

Joe Kennedy lived to bring up four fine sons . . . and to see three of them die: Joe Jr. and John (standing right and left of their father) and Bobby (seated right). Now only Teddy (above right) remains to fulfil his dream.

stuck in her windpipe. While her children watched in wide-eyed horror she choked to death.

But Ethel's cruellest loss was still to come . . .

Bobby himself never forgot John's death. The memory of those horrifying minutes in Dallas was etched permanently on his face, in his eyes. On the third anniversary of the assassination Ethel was forced to invite some friends to play tennis with her husband to try to rouse him from his depression.

Politically, Bobby grew stronger and stronger. In many quarters he was disliked, considered to be 'ruthless' and an 'opportunist,' but he had friends as well.

Always a devoted husband and father, he became even more of a family man after John's death, and his rambling home at Hickory Hill was always alive with children—not just his own but children of friends and neighbors too. He loved children.

By November 1967 Bobby was leading the popularity polls over President Johnson by 52 to 32. And the people who believed he had 'many of the same outstanding qualities of JFK' had risen from 49 percent to 54 percent in less than six months. His strongest support seemed to come from among women and young people.

Popperfoto

Almost without his intending it to happen, Bobby's destiny was pointing him towards the White House, along the same route as his dead brother. And he was just as dedicated. Asked once whether politics was worth the strain, the stress and the risk involved, he replied, "No sacrifices are involved. I might say it is the only reason for being alive."

At the beginning of 1968, Bobby got up in the Senate and declared, "I am announcing today my candidacy for the presidency of the United States." It was an uncanny moment for those who had been there eight years previously and heard John F. Kennedy utter the same words. Here was another Kennedy throwing in his lot, his life, for his country. Shortly afterwards President Johnson announced he would not seek re-election.

Footprints

Now Bobby hit the campaign trail with all the customary Kennedy intensity. His reception varied from town to town but he seldom met with indifference. Some people loved him for being a Kennedy, some hated him. But the family footprints were deep. He campaigned for the poor, the black, for Vietnam and for Israel. He was strongly pro-Israel and announced that America was "committed to Israel's survival . . ." They were words which may have cost him more than votes.

In a small house in Pasadena, Southern California, a young Jordanian Arab called Sirhan Sirhan seethed. As a child in 1948 he had been uprooted by the Arab-Israeli war, the same war that Bobby Kennedy had covered admiringly from the front-line as a correspondent for the Boston 'Post'.

Sirhan's hatred of Israel increased when the Jews won the six-day war on June 5, 1967. In a secret journal Sirhan noted the "necessity to assassinate Senator Kennedy" before the first anniversary of the war.

Bobby Kennedy knew the risks of following his brother's presidential path. He once admitted, "I know there will be an attempt on my life sooner or later. Not so much for political reasons but through contagion, through emulation." He refused to be guarded by uniformed police and his only protection were his personal aides who tried to keep as close to him as possible in public.

On June 4, the day California went to the polls, Bobby Kennedy's bandwagon had reached Los Angeles. It was a busy day ending up at the Ambassador Hotel where Kennedy gave a speech thanking his 2000 campaign workers for their support and dedication.

By now it seemed pretty certain that Bobby was going to carry California, and

the mood of the campaigners was one of elation.

At 12.16 a.m. in the morning of June 5 Kennedy was on his way down from the hotel's Embassy Room to the Colonial Room to talk to the overflow of his campaign workers. He was then to go to a private party at 'The Factory,' a fashionable night-club and then, next morning, on to Chicago.

Because of the congestion outside the main door of the ballroom Kennedy left through the back way, striding down towards the kitchens. With him was his wife Ethel, pregnant for the eleventh time, a close friend Roosevelt Grier who was a member of the Los Angeles Rams professional football team, and three other close aides. Bobby Kennedy moved through the delighted crowd, through the cheers and congratulations, through the wall of outstretched hands.

One of the hands belonged to Sirhan Sirhan. And it held an Iver Johnson pistol. Seconds later Bobby Kennedy was lying wide-eyed on his back, blood gushing out of a head wound, surrounded by the distraught people who loved him. At least two of the eight shots had found their mark, one behind his right ear, one in his right armpit.

In seconds the mood had changed from victory to grief. "Oh, no! It can't be! Not *again!*" A radio reporter gasped, "Senator Kennedy has been shot! Is that possible? Is that possible?"

In Hyannis Port, Massachusetts, three hours ahead of Californian time, Rose Kennedy awoke early to go to mass, switched on the television to catch California's final results and learned that her son was on his way to hospital.

All Over Again

"It seemed impossible that the same kind of disaster could befall our family twice in five years," she later wrote. "If I had read anything of the sort in fiction I would have put it aside as incredible." On the way to church Rose Kennedy kept thinking "Oh, Bobby, Bobby, Bobby." She still had not passed on the sad news to her sleeping husband.

In San Francisco, Ted Kennedy also learned about the shooting from his television set. He telephoned Hyannis Port and broke the news to his crippled father, for the second time in his life.

At the Good Samaritan Hospital in Los Angeles Bobby underwent brain surgery. It lasted three hours and 45 minutes and even when it was completed doctors had no idea how much of his brain would remain as before—even if he survived.

For 25 hours Bobby's life hovered on a precipice. At 1.44 a.m. on June 6 he slipped quietly over the edge. Said an unrepentant Sirhan Sirhan, "I did it for my country."

Popperfoto

"We love you Bobby!" When he took on his brother's political mantle, huge crowds welcomed him. But there was one man who hated all he stood for: minutes after a rousing speech to his supporters Bobby was gunned down by Sirhan.

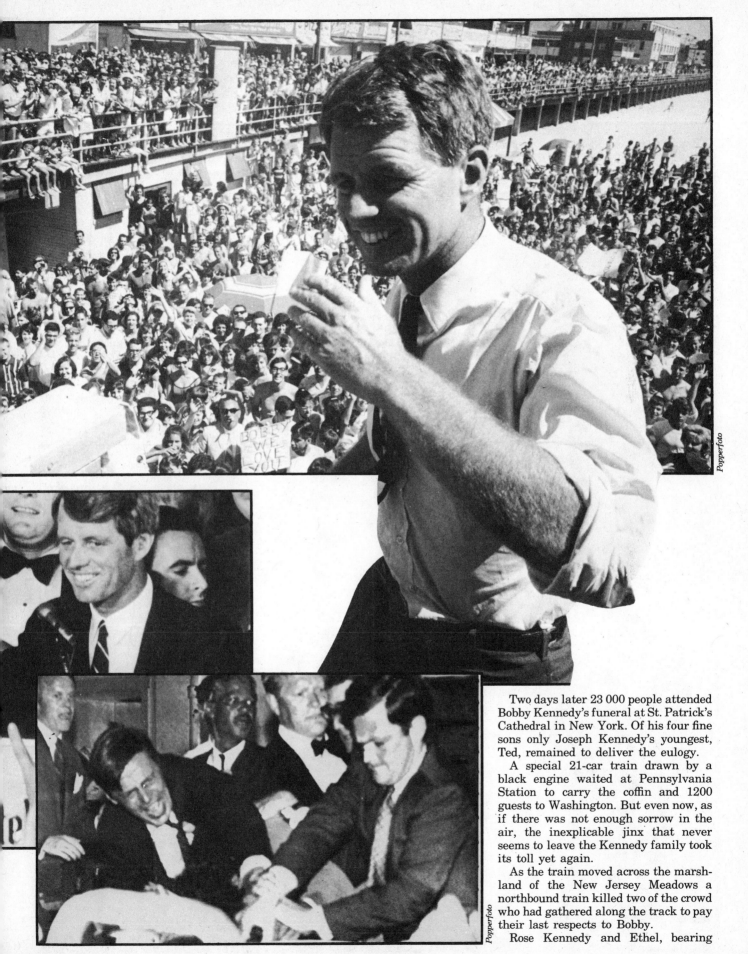

Popperfoto

Popperfoto

Two days later 23 000 people attended Bobby Kennedy's funeral at St. Patrick's Cathedral in New York. Of his four fine sons only Joseph Kennedy's youngest, Ted, remained to deliver the eulogy.

A special 21-car train drawn by a black engine waited at Pennsylvania Station to carry the coffin and 1200 guests to Washington. But even now, as if there was not enough sorrow in the air, the inexplicable jinx that never seems to leave the Kennedy family took its toll yet again.

As the train moved across the marsh-land of the New Jersey Meadows a northbound train killed two of the crowd who had gathered along the track to pay their last respects to Bobby.

Rose Kennedy and Ethel, bearing

inside her Bobby's last child, the baby he would never see, carried themselves with the traditional calm and dignity of the Kennedy women through their all-too-frequent bereavements. John's widow, Jackie, rejoined the clan to mourn the brother-in-law who had been such a strength to her in her grief.

But it was Bobby's oldest son, Joe III, aged 15, who set the mourners a glowing example of the Kennedy courage. Joe had adored his father. Now, head erect, he walked the length of the funeral train shaking hands with everyone aboard. "I'm Joe Kennedy. Thank you for coming. Thank you for your sympathy. Thank you."

Bobby Kennedy was 42 when he died. He was buried in Arlington, by candlelight, just a few feet away from his brother John whose life—and death—his had followed so closely.

The only mourner missing was his father, Joseph, who at 79 had outlived four of his children. Paralyzed from a stroke, he was too distraught to make the sad journey. Once again his dream of

Eight years after his death, Bobby's family visit his grave: Rory—who never knew him—brings roses.

greatness for the Kennedy name had ended in tears.

Of all his children Joseph Kennedy felt Bobby resembled him most. He once said, "Jack has always been one to persuade people to do things. Bobby tends to tell people what to do. He's a great kid—he hates the same way I do."

But Bobby could also love. He had a disarming, almost shy, charm. And he could laugh at himself. Campaigning in Sioux Falls, South Dakota, he was asked what priority he would give the Sioux Falls economy if he was elected president. "Top priority," he replied. "Just this morning at breakfast I said to Ethel, 'We've got to do something about the Sioux Falls economy.'" The wry humor was classic Bobby Kennedy.

It was Bobby Kennedy who, of all the sons, seemed most concerned that the family name should endure. He felt passionately that it was his duty to carry on what his brother began. "Men," he said, "are not made for safe havens."

For Ethel Kennedy his murder was the culmination of 13 years of violent premature deaths. This time the blow was more than she could handle. This time she was barely able to control her grief. Bobby had been her whole life and

with him gone it was as if she had nothing left to live for. After the funeral she seemed unable to face her own company. She kept insisting on playing frantic games of tennis, dashing around the court, forcing herself on and on.

She installed a juke box in her garage which she played loudly all night long, constantly filling her home with people and parties to deaden her mind to the harsh reality. One day she fell, exhausted, on the tennis court, and the family were fearful she would lose the baby that was not long due.

Ethel and Jackie became closer, drawn together by their mutual tragedies, and would spend afternoons talking together. But Jackie never joined in any of Ethel's parties.

Finally Rory Kennedy was born, eleventh and last of Bobby Kennedy's children. Her inheritance is one of glory and tragedy. Of triumph and sudden death.

Her father once said, "Politics can hurt badly but there are lots of other ways of getting hurt in life." As a Kennedy, Bobby had more than his share of hurts. He carried them with him to his grave. But for the family who survived him the legacy of grief continued. . . .

U.P.I.

The Mythmakers

Don't be beastly to the humans

It took a long time for 'space art' to work its way round to showing aliens as cuddly creatures. But gradually, the grabbing tentacles gave way to a Martian handshake...

1934: a lump of cosmic blubber.
1930: a sea-food cocktail.
1936: animated pin-pong balls.

Things had to become worse before they could get better; that seems to have been the philosophy of the science fiction illustrators of the 1930s, with their emphasis on ever-more-revolting 'creatures from outer space'.

Bug-eyed humanoids were left behind in their gallery of intergalactic gargoyles. The intrepid Earthman who ventured on to the cover of any science fiction magazine now risked being entwined in the tentacles of some rampaging lump of cosmic blubber—as in Jack Williams's 1934 spine-chiller —gobbled up by an outsize sea-anemone (*Amazing Stories*, November 1930) or treated as a cocktail snack by a cross between a lobster and a sentient ping-pong ball (*Astounding*, June 1936).

In the summer 1938 edition of *Tales of Wonder*, artist W. J. Roberts even saw human beings kept as slaves by a race of lizard-like amphibious aliens with a weakness for sunbathing on the beach with the captured females. The result wasn't quite so chilling as Roberts intended. The illustration looks hilariously like the cover of an interplanetary holiday-brochure.

Anthony Frewin

Anthony Frewin

Life was harder for the cosmonauts —as if it wasn't enough to conquer weightlessness, the time barrier, lack of oxygen, extreme temperatures and the fact that there might not even be a return ticket home.

But as they kept a firm grip on their ray-guns and their eyes fixed bravely in the direction of the cover price, things were beginning to improve.

In the 1940s a new element started to appear in space art. Having overcome

85

TALES OF WONDER

N°3

1/-

THE HORROR
IN THE
TELESCOPE
BY
EDMOND HAMILTON

LIFE ON JUPITER

Jupiter's inhabitants would need to be massive, of tremendous strength to cope with the enormous gravity of this giant world. They would probably be forced to a clumsy means of locomotion, since long legs would be impossible. An Earthman would need a tractor car to get about!

For complete details, see page 97
FANTASTIC ADVENTURES, JANUARY 1940

Anthony Frewin

their initial hostility, the aliens were beginning to become friendly.

Of course, they looked just as bizarre, but their intentions were noticeably more peaceful. The 'breakthrough' began in 1939 with Frank Paul's interpretations of what creatures conditioned by life on specific planets might look like.

The aliens of Jupiter, one learned, would 'need to be massive, with tremendous strength, to cope with the enormous gravity' and lo! there they were, crowding round the earthly astronauts' tractor like herds of inquisitive seals.

By the time our astronauts had reached Uranus (three issues later, give

**1938: its a hard life in the cosmic corps. Off-duty aliens relaxing.
1939: Verisimilitude rears its ugly head. Could they look like this?
1939: Hands across the cosmos. We're really all the same—under the spacesuit.
1939: Entente cordiale, or how to win friends and influence aliens.**

LIFE ON URANUS

the MAN from MARS

by PAUL

or take a few million light-years) the aliens were almost in a party mood, inviting them down into their subterranean world with quite delightfully coy and toothy smiles.

The climax in interplanetary understanding came with Paul's conception of a Martian—looking like an undernourished hippy in a sheepskin jacket—solemnly shaking hands with an Earthman, while still cautiously clinging to his 'atom rifle,' just in case we couldn't be trusted.

Of course, this lull in hostilities couldn't last.

Maybe an alien had got his hands on a copy of *Playboy* magazine, carelessly left lying in an earthly spacecraft. Maybe one of our astronauts had whispered something in a Martian ear. Whatever the reason, their friendliness suddenly took an intense and aggressive turn. They had discovered sex.

ROMANCE
THAT ROCKED AN EMPIRE

King Edward VIII of England was still a bachelor at 36. Then he met Wallis Simpson, a worldly American society beauty. It could have been an ideal match. But Mrs Simpson was not only married, she had already divorced one husband. Under a cloak of secrecy, the official reaction was made clear to Edward . . . 'This woman can never be Queen'. But the King had other ideas.

Popperfoto

At a little after three o'clock in the afternoon of November 17, 1936, Miss Ellen Wilkinson, a socialist Member of the British Parliament, rose in her place on the Opposition benches of the House of Commons to put a brief question to Sir Walter Runciman, the President of the Board of Trade.

Taking care to employ the proper mode of address to a Government Minister, on which the Commons has always insisted, Miss Wilkinson asked, "Can the Right Honorable Gentleman say why, in the case of two American magazines of the highest repute imported into this country in the last few weeks, two and sometimes three pages have been torn out, and what is this thing that the British public are not allowed to know?"

The reply by the President of the Board of Trade was even shorter than the question. "My department," he said, "has nothing to do with that."

Miss Wilkinson knew perfectly well why pages had been removed from the magazines—*Time* and *Newsweek*—and so did every one of her fellow Members of Parliament, every Peer of the Realm, sitting in the adjoining chamber of the House of Lords, and every journalist in Fleet Street, the center of Britain's national press. Many other prominent people in business, the churches, in the great financial institutions of the City of London and in well-to-do 'society' also knew the reason, Miss Wilkinson was simply making a forlorn attempt to lift the veil from the secret that was being so assiduously kept from the mass of the British people, even to the extent of expunging any hint of it from imported foreign magazines: the secret that King Edward VIII, who had so recently succeeded his dead father, George V, intended to marry an American divorcée, Mrs Wallis Warfield Simpson.

All well-informed people in London's tight-knit influential groups also knew that the proprietors of Britain's national newspapers had entered into a 'gentleman's agreement' to withhold news of Edward's 'affair' with Wallis for fear that premature disclosure would create a constitutional crisis of unprecedented magnitude.

The most fearful man in Britain was the country's 69-year-old Prime Minister, Stanley Baldwin. Nothing, in his view, was more likely to undermine Britain's impeccably respectable monarchy, and destroy the allegiance of Colonies and Dominions to the British Empire itself, than that Edward should marry a twice-divorced American commoner and make her his Queen. Secrecy, he argued, must be maintained until the perverse Edward had been dissuaded from his passion for Wallis Simpson. The Baldwin government faced what Queen Mary, Edward's mother, had so quaintly described as 'a nice kettle of fish'.

That was putting it all too mildly. For what Queen Mary did not know was that Edward was already hinting darkly that he *would* marry Wallis Simpson, come what may, and even if that meant that he was left with no alternative but to abandon his throne. The dreadful, whispered word was Abdication.

First Meeting

Stanley Baldwin had bitter cause to regret that day, back in the winter of 1931, when Edward, then 36 and still the Prince of Wales, had first met Wallis Simpson. She and her husband, Ernest, had been guests at a dinner party at Fort Belvedere, the Prince's favorite royal residence set among spacious grounds near the banks of the River Thames, 30 miles from London. The Simpsons were strangers to the Prince, introduced to him by a mutual friend.

At their first meeting, Edward and Wallis exchanged no more than a few words. He, by way of encouraging conversation, suggested that, as an American, she probably regretted the absence of central heating in coldly damp Britain. She, in rather daringly mocking tones, replied that her royal host had disappointed her, for "every woman who comes to your country is always asked the same question. I had hoped for something more original from the Prince of Wales!"

That light-hearted comment, with its subtle indications of a strongly independent personality, stuck in Edward's

The head-on conflict between Prime Minister and King threatened to disrupt the government. Wallis Simpson, who had captured the king's heart, found that Baldwin's was turned stonily against her.

Popperfoto

John Frost

Daily Mirror
THE DAILY PICTURE NEWSPAPER WITH THE LARGEST NET SALE

SATURDAY
Dec. 5, No. 10361
ONE PENNY

GOD SAVE THE KING!

TELL US THE FACTS, MR. BALDWIN!

"Suggestions have appeared that if the King decided to marry, his wife need not become Queen. These ideas are without any constitutional foundation.

"There is no such thing as what is called a morganatic marriage known to our law. The Royal Marriages Act of 1772 has no application to the Sovereign himself.

"This Act, therefore, has nothing to do with the present case. The King himself requires no consent from any other authority to make his marriage legal, but, as I have said, the lady whom he marries by the *fact* of her marriage to the King necessarily becomes Queen.

"She herself therefore enjoys all the status, rights, and privileges which, both by positive law and by custom, attach to that position ... and her children would be in the direct line of succession to the throne.

"The only possible way in which this result could be avoided would be by legislation dealing with a particular case. His Majesty's Government are not prepared to introduce such legislation.

"Such a change could not be effective without the consent of all the Dominions. I am satisfied from inquiries I have made that this assent would not be forthcoming."
— MR. BALDWIN IN PARLIAMENT YESTERDAY.

THE NATION INSISTS ON KNOWING THE KING'S FULL DEMANDS AND CONDITIONS

The Country Will Give You the Verdict

mind and caused him to pay increasing attention to Wallis when, soon after the Fort Belvedere dinner, he began regularly to entertain his new-found friends, the Simpsons.

Wallis Simpson, at the time, was 35. She had been born and raised in Baltimore, Maryland, the only child of a marriage that had united two of America's oldest Colonial families, the Warfields of Maryland and the Montagues of Virginia. At 20 she had married Earl Winfield Spencer Jr., a lieutenant in the United States Navy's aviation corps, but she had discovered him to be an alcoholic and after a long separation, while he was posted to the Far East and she remained at home, she had divorced him in December 1927.

Seven months after that divorce, Wallis married Ernest Simpson, a New Yorker by birth, who had left Harvard before graduating to join the British Coldstream Guards, and had later become a British citizen. Wallis had met Simpson in London, where he had his stockbroking business, and it was in London's 'society' center, Mayfair, that the couple settled after a romantic honeymoon tour through France and Spain.

Social Charisma

Wallis Simpson emerged as the ideal Mayfair hostess, intelligent and charming, elegant and graceful, and a superb organizer of entertaining dinner parties characterized by memorable Southern cooking on which she had become an expert. Normally, London's 1930s social 'set' erected near-impenetrable barriers against strangers, and especially 'foreigners,' and it was entirely due to Wallis's personal charisma that she and her husband were quickly 'accepted.'

Within three years of the introductory dinner party at Fort Belvedere, Ernest and Wallis Simpson had become acknowledged members of the Prince of Wales' private 'court'. They visited nightclubs with the Prince and were regularly included in his party for evenings at the theater or opera. Increasingly, it was observed, Mrs Simpson took a 'supervisory' interest in the Prince. On one occasion she gently reprimanded him for the inelegance of carrying a cigar in the breast pocket of his jacket. She would herself suggest the menus for meals at Fort Belvedere when she felt that those offered by the chefs were insufficiently adventurous.

Ernest Simpson, however, was less enthusiastic about the London party-going round than Wallis. He was a man with intellectual interests who much preferred the quiet of an evening at home to the noisy, boisterous atmosphere of the nightclubs, and a stimulating book rather than the banalities of

Popperfoto

Mr Ernest Simpson, an American who had taken up British citizenship, chivalrously gave his wife Wallis grounds for divorce so that she was free to marry.

dinner-table smalltalk. Despite the fact that he and the Prince had become good friends, Ernest Simpson began to decline more social invitations than he accepted. David—as Edward was always known to family and friends—accepted Mr. Simpson's apologies for absence with good grace and continued to enjoy the companionship of Mrs Simpson.

It was quite clear that the bachelor Prince was maturing socially under the guidance of the more sophisticated Wallis Simpson, and that he found her company infinitely more engaging than that of most of the people with whom he was obliged to associate in official court circles. So far as London's social chessboard was concerned, Wallis Simpson had been assigned to the dominating role of 'Queen'. Indeed, as one observant American journalist told her readers, Mrs Simpson's invitations as a hostess had come to 'rank as commands. Her position in London is without precedent for an American'. It was also without precedent in Edward's private, emotional life and in the months that preceded the death of his father, George V—in January 1936—the Prince had come to realize that he was deeply in love with Wallis.

Vital Introduction

One of the most crucial dates in the whole Edward and Wallis saga was undoubtedly May 27, 1936. That evening Edward—now Edward VIII—held a small, select dinner party at St. James's Palace, London, at which those around the table included Colonel and Mrs Charles A. Lindbergh, Mr and Mrs Stanley Baldwin and Wallis and Ernest Simpson—who, on this occasion, had been faced with an invitation that he could hardly refuse. On the face of it, the occasion was simply an opportunity for the new King to surround himself with knowledgeable and 'interesting' people. In reality, Edward had stage-managed it for a very specific, personal reason: he wished Stanley Baldwin to meet Mrs Simpson in a relaxed, informal atmosphere in the hope that the Prime Minister would respond to her natural charm and so be amenably 'conditioned' for the course on which the King was determined to embark.

In the event, the King's plan went totally awry. Baldwin could find no common ground with Mrs Simpson and, in any case, his anger and disapproval of the tittle-tattled love affair had nurtured a deeply-rooted prejudice against her. It was not easy for him to mind his manners, sitting at the same table with the lady and her husband and remembering how George V, to whose ears gossip had reached, had cried out shortly before his death, "After I am dead the boy will ruin himself in twelve months!"

Edward, however, was as tenacious as his Prime Minister was obdurate. On July 9 he arranged another dinner at which the 18 guests included Mr and Mrs Winston Churchill and Wallis Simpson, on her own. The following day the King ordered the guest list to be printed in the *Court Circular,* the official public 'diary' of royal events which was automatically reproduced in *The Times* and other leading London newspapers. The name 'Mrs Ernest Simpson' appeared, almost casually, last on the list but it was read by Baldwin and others, as Edward intended it should be, as a declaration of defiance.

Hotel de Paris

Just 12 days after that announcement Ernest Simpson booked into the comfortable Hotel de Paris, in the Thames-side village of Bray, some four miles west of Windsor Castle, and there spent the night with a woman who, according to a subsequent legal document, was adorned with the name of Buttercup Kennedy. In due course Wallis wrote the following note to her husband:

"Dear Ernest: I have just learned that while you have been away, instead of being on business as you led me to believe, you have been staying at an hotel at Bray with a lady. I am sure you must realize that this is conduct which I cannot possibly overlook and I must insist that you do not continue to live with me. This only confirms suspicions which I have had for a long time. I am therefore instructing my solicitors to take proceedings for a divorce. Wallis."

Meanwhile, the King had decided that he needed a holiday and in the 1600-ton, luxuriously-appointed motor yacht *Nahlin*—chartered from its millionaire owner, Lady Yule—he set off to cruise the Mediterranean and the Adriatic. With him traveled his personal 'courtiers' and Wallis Simpson. At every port of call the King and his party were mobbed by enthusiastic crowds. Edward and Wallis were photographed in Yugoslavia, walking hand-in-hand; they were filmed swimming together in a quiet Adriatic bay. American and European newspapers reported avidly upon their progress and, in the United States, headline writers blessed the accommodating manner in which the words 'KING AND WALLY' could be captured in the very largest typefaces.

Yet, to the general British public, the presence in *Nahlin* of Mrs Simpson remained a tightly-clamped secret. They were told only that the King was combining a holiday with official engagements. (He did, in fact, pay brief duty calls on Prince Paul of Yugoslavia and King George of Greece.) But there was no mention of Mrs Simpson in the British newspapers and only photographs showing the King alone, or with one of his 'acceptable' male guests, were used.

At the end of the cruise the King returned briefly to London and then went north to the Scottish highlands for a two-week stay at Balmoral Castle. To join him there he summoned a clutch of dukes and duchesses—and Wallis Simpson.

There, too, he made a grievous blunder that did much to exacerbate the hostility towards him which was gathering force around Baldwin and the Prime Minister's closest colleagues. He suddenly canceled a long-standing appointment to open a new wing of an Aberdeen hospital, 60 miles from Balmoral, on the plea that he was still in mourning for his father and could not yet undertake public duties. Yet, on the day on which he should have been received by the deeply hurt and disappointed City Fathers, he was seen at the local railway station effusively greeting Mrs Simpson.

Within the privacy of Balmoral, the dominant topic of discussion between the two lovers was Mrs Simpson's forthcoming suit for divorce. She had already rented a small house in the English eastern county of Suffolk so that her case could be heard in the courthouse of the county town of Ipswich, 72 miles from London. Whether her advisers hoped to avoid public attention, or were motivated by the fact that the waiting lists for divorce cases were much shorter outside the capital, was never clear. If they were hoping for no publicity, then they were due for considerable disappointment.

On the day of the case, October 27, Mrs Simpson was driven from her temporary Suffolk home to Ipswich by George Ladbrook, the King's own personal chauffeur. She arrived to find the courthouse surrounded by townspeople in apparently festive mood. Somehow, by means of some grapevine—no doubt assisted by the inside knowledge of the hordes of American journalists who had descended on the town—everyone in the crowd seemed to know Mrs Simpson's name and was also aware, at least in some vague way, that she had 'something to do with the King.'

The few British newspapermen from London's Fleet Street hovered near the courthouse doors in chastened mood. They already knew that, at the end of the day, all that they could write would be one paragraph saying that an unknown Mrs Ernest Simpson had secured a divorce (or failed to secure, as the court might decide) from an obscure Mr Ernest Simpson.

The courthouse security measures, arbitrarily imposed by the authorities, were such that had never before been seen in what was supposed to be merely another divorce case involving totally private citizens. Police ringed the build-

Popperfoto

"The King and Wally" provided fascinating fodder for the world's newspapers during their holiday together cruising the Mediterranean. But, when this picture was taken (August 1936, at Tregir), the British press was still debarred from printing gossip about the love affair—though it was common knowledge among journalists.

ing and one embarrassed local constable was obliged to stop the town's Mayor from entering until he had produced an official pass. Only 30 reporters, bearing first-come-first-served tickets, were admitted and when they finally squeezed into the courtroom they found that the seating had been rearranged so that reporters and public saw only the backs of witnesses and not their faces.

King's Counsel

The judge, Sir John Hawke, took his seat at exactly 2.17 p.m. and Norman Birkett, King's Counsel and one of the great luminaries of the English Bar, at once called his client, Mrs. Simpson. Gently he led her through the history of her married life. She had lived happily with her husband until the autumn of 1934? She had, she said, in a clear, firm voice with an accent that some locals designated as 'just slightly American'.

Then, asked Mr Birkett (employing that unique lawyers' cadence which seems to imply that the question is ridiculously obvious but must be put), did her husband's manner change? Yes, it did, Wallis agreed. "He was indifferent, and often went away week-ends."

At Birkett's request she read her 'Dear Ernest' note and then stepped down to make way for members of the staff of Bray's Hotel de Paris. They confirmed that an English cup of tea had been Mr Simpson's undoing. It was taken up to his room and there beside him, in the double bed, was a lady whom chambermaids and others could now testify was certainly not Mrs Simpson.

Sir John Hawke could at times be testy and this day he was plainly irritated. It was clear that he, at least, believed that his court had been saddled with the case simply in the hope of evading publicity and he was not at all pleased. He was even less happy with the evidence being put before him.

Courts at the time were being inundated with what English lawyers referred to, mysteriously, as 'ordinary hotel evidence' but which was merely a euphemism for collusion—an agreement between the parties to end a marriage, with the husband chivalrously undertaking to be 'discovered' in a hotel bed with a woman who offered her services for the occasion.

The prevalence of such cases was almost wholly due to the fact that in Britain the stringent divorce laws of the time made adultery practically the sole grounds for ending a marriage. Since incompatibility was regarded as frivolous and unacceptable, adultery had to be 'arranged'. Such cases could often be pinpointed by the fact that the name of the woman was 'unknown' but, in this instance, as Mr Birkett was swift to point out, the lady had been named in

THE DAILY MIRROR, Friday, December 4, 1936

Daily Mirror
THE DAILY PICTURE NEWSPAPER WITH THE LARGEST NET SALE

FRIDAY
Dec. 4 No. 10300
ONE PENNY

Registered at the G.P.O. as a newspaper

			FILMS · · · · 24	AMUSEMENTS	BROADCASTING · · 18	
JANE · · · · Page 21	HOME PAGE · · · 27	SERIAL AND FIFE · 22	DOROTHY DIX · · 26	PIP & SQUEAK · · 20	
BELINDA · · · · 26	RUGGLES · · · · 29				

THE KING SEES THE PREMIER LAST NIGHT: HOPE OF SETTLEMENT GROWS

THE KING SPENT LAST NIGHT AT BUCKINGHAM PALACE. THE PRIME MINISTER, MR. BALDWIN, DROVE THERE AT 9.15 AND FOR THE SECOND SUCCESSIVE DAY HAD A GRAVE TALK ON THE KING'S DESIRE TO MARRY MRS. SIMPSON, AND THE SERIOUS CONSTITUTIONAL CRISIS IT HAS CAUSED.

MR. Baldwin travelled in a closed car, driving through the garden entrance, which is usually reserved for kings and those of royal blood. He was at once shown to the King's apartment and stayed fifty minutes. His face was grave as he left.

At 10.40 the King left the Palace for Marlborough House to see Queen Mary. Earlier in the evening, on his return from Fort Belvedere, the King had seen Queen Mary at Marlborough House. His visit was revealed in the Court Circular.

Soon afterwards the Royal Family assembled at Marlborough House to discuss the situation. The Queen, the Duke and Duchess of York, the Duke and Duchess of Gloucester and the Duke of Kent were present.

The emphatic view of all, it is understood, was that the King must not abdicate.

Lords and Commons

Meet To-day

To-day momentous decisions are expected to be made. The House of Lords, which only meets Friday in unusual circumstances, has been called for 11 a.m. The House of Commons is also sitting and a statement is expected to be made simultaneously in both Houses.

It is believed that an understanding between the Ministers and the Crown on the King's wish to marry is imminent.

A compromise satisfactory both to the throne and Empire may be reached.

The Daily Mirror understands that when the crisis is ended the King will most probably broadcast to his people.

The King has a sure instinct in these matters and there is no doubt that there is nothing his millions of subjects will appreciate more than hearing from the King's own lips how he reached the most momentous decision of his life.

Long Talk by Telephone

While crowds waited outside her London home in Cumberland-terrace, Regent's Park, last evening, Mrs. Simpson had a long telephone talk with the King who was then at Fort Belvedere.

She motored down to Fort Belvedere shortly after the King's car left for Buckingham

(Continued on back page)

U.S. GOVERNMENT MAY ADVISE MRS. SIMPSON

FROM OUR OWN CORRESPONDENT

REPORTS on the train in Britain and Mrs. Simpson's part in it are being made to Washington by Mr. W. Bingham, the American Ambassador in London.

It is considered here that Mrs. Simpson is entitled to any assistance and advice the American Government authorities in London can give her.

As the Washington State Department has never been advised of her formal renunciation of American citizenship, they regard her both as a subject of Britain and a citizen of the United States.

On presenting her old American passport to any other consuls-general's department in London, the Consuls-General's department in London can claim that her maintenance in Britain ... that real nationality will remain until the renounces one or the other.

This is her right, as through the Act of 1922 American women who marry foreigners do not lose their citizenship unless they formally renounce it.

the divorce petition.

Sir John Hawke seemed as much unable to throw off his annoyance as the head cold that was troubling him. "Well, I suppose I must come to the conclusion that there was adultery in this case," he grumbled, and agreed to grant a *decree nisi*. (That meant that, unless—*nisi* —circumstances changed within the then-statutory waiting period of six months, the divorce would become final.)

Costs, Mr Birkett politely inquired, would be charged against the respondent (Ernest Simpson)? "Yes," Sir John replied, even more lugubriously, "costs against the respondent, I'm afraid. I suppose I must in these unusual circumstances. So you may have it with costs."

Thus it was, in a hearing lasting not quite 20 minutes, that Mrs Simpson secured a decree which, by the following May, would become absolute and then leave her free to remarry. The King himself heard the news with relief. He now saw no reason why he should depart from his total commitment to marry Wallis Simpson and make her his Queen —in royal authority as well as in name.

Baldwin saw it all so differently. He made a hasty calculation and came up with the alarming answer that Mrs Simpson would be legally entitled to

When the news broke in Britain, the newspapers showed sympathy for the pair.

marry Edward, if the King wished it, two weeks *before* his Coronation. (A new monarch officially ascends the throne at the moment of his predecessor's death but the actual crowning follows later.)

Would the King try to marry without his Minister's approval? No-one could be sure. Embarrassed constitutional lawyers were forced to admit that they could produce no definitive answer. One thing was certain: the Church of England was implacably opposed to divorce, although obliged to tolerate it in lesser persons. Even 'innocent parties' were still regarded as somehow tainted and among older people, in all social classes, divorce carried an indelible social stigma.

But the especially terrible thing for Baldwin was that the King might try to marry a woman who had divorced not once but *twice*—and who had two husbands living. As the Prime Minister saw it, the hands of the British constitutional clock stood at five minutes to midnight and he was determined that when the bell tolled it should be for Edward and Wallis and not for Stanley Baldwin and the British Government.

MRS. SIMPSON—a portrait taken recently —Exclusive to the "Daily Mirror"

THE CRISIS—FROM EVERY ANGLE

	Page
See us at Fort Belvedere and Downing-street	3 and 4
Parliament and the Crisis	
What the World Thinks	
Coronation Orders Held	
The Story of Mrs. Simpson	14, 16, 17, 19 and 22
The Man in the Street's View	
Public Opinion and the King	
Picture	
It CAN Happen Here!	
Effect in the City	

John Frost

OUR NEW HOME AMONG THE STARS

Suspended magically between the Earth and the Moon is a gigantic 'wheel' where a colony of human beings are beginning a new life away from all earthly problems. In their 'Space City' of rivers, gardens, skiing resorts and sun-warmed beaches, they fly like birds, alter their surroundings at the touch of a switch, even play 'three-dimensional baseball'. Unbridled fantasy? No, say the scientists, this is how millions of us may be living before the end of next century in the greatest 'emigration' experiment of all time.

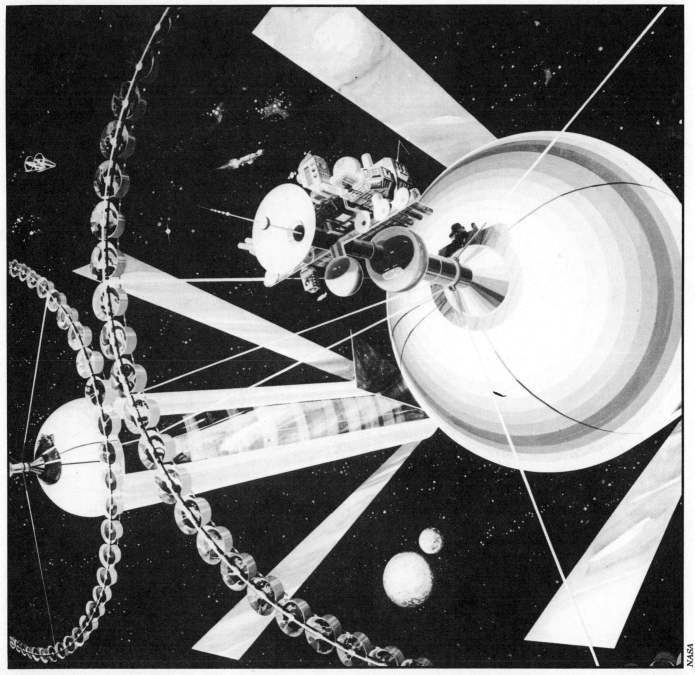

NASA

Eta woke early. Outside her home, all was darkness except for the streetlights of a township in the valley and the necklace of blue and red lights which traced the path of the monorail.

She checked the time—05.29.37. Even as she watched, a soft orange glow broke the darkness on the horizon and fingers of golden light crept across the strangely curving landscape.

Though Eta and her husband had spent three years in this artificial world, it was always a thrilling moment when the petal-like louvres opened on the sides of their immense city—like some vast, mechanical flower—to admit the light of a new day. She never could resist the sight of Mother Earth rising between green hills in the velvet black of space.

It may sound like science-fiction, a dream of the future, but distinguished scientists in the United States believe that the first city in Space may be a *reality* before the middle of the next century.

This is not just a matter of speculation. Many of the details have been worked out already . . . heralding what could become a 'paradise city' suspended in space, colonized by thousands of people from Earth, living in perfect conditions where overcrowding, pollution, disease, violence, hunger and even boredom have been banished.

The ultimate 'City in the Sky' would not be a sterile, antiseptic place, as inhuman as a hospital corridor. The 'Cosmic Colony' could be made to simulate almost any earthly conditions you like, almost at the touch of a button. Snow-capped 'mountains', palm-fringed beaches, lakes and meadows, all can be recreated and controlled. In this wonderful 'New World', all the worst and ugliest elements of our own Earth would have been eliminated.

Imagine two immense cylinders—each 19 miles long and four miles wide—coupled by tension cables and spinning like tops once every 114 seconds to create artificial gravity. The dome-like end-caps enclose a reduced-pressure oxygen-nitrogen atmosphere. At the extreme end of the cylinders are dish-shaped mirrors which provide the colony with solar power. The spinning 'habitats'—the name scientists give the living area—constantly face the Sun.

Inside, a whole new world has blossomed.

Huge 'solars'—seemingly endless glass windows—run almost the entire length of the cylinder. Natural sunlight is reflected from enormous rectangular mirrors and shines through the 'solars' on to the extraordinary scene below.

The curved 'valleys' of the cylinder have been 'landscaped' to recreate an Earth-like panorama of rolling meadows and hills, parklands and forests. Townships are spread through the valleys to give the colonists the greatest possible 'elbow room' and freedom of movement. Centrifugal force—substituting for gravity—would mean you would have your feet planted firmly on the ground.

The interior environment, with its luxuriant vegetation, would give an immediate feeling of naturalness and warmth, as distinct from the hard and metallic appearance of a conventional space station.

From the 'end-cap' of the cylinder you would get an awesome impression of the simulated Earth-like conditions, with their lakes, rivers, hills and woodland. The large, movable, rectangular mirrors at the far end of each cylinder direct sunlight into the interior, and movable louvres artificially regulate the 'seasons' and control the day-night cycle.

Controlled Environment

Overhead, the sky is blue, clouds form naturally and—just to make you feel 'at home'—there is occasional light rainfall. In this 'greenhouse' environment, plants—including food crops—play a vital part in the life cycle, supplying food and returning oxygen to the air.

Colonies of this size could provide a perfectly controlled home for more than a million people. Everything a human being could possibly need would be cultivated or produced within the colony, an improvement on Earth itself.

Slowly revolving around the cylinder in the opposite direction would be a ring of 'tea-cup' containers. These would be agricultural stations, supplying the colony with animal and fish protein, wheat, corn, maize, fruit and other products.

Gourmets among the colonizers needn't worry about being fed with processed food. Some of the containers would be adapted as fish-farms, breeding everything from fresh salmon to oysters.

The inhabitants would need a high-energy diet, for the main purpose of the colony would be to utilize the vast mineral resources of the Moon. Although non-polluting light industry could be carried on inside the main cylinders, near the townships, the great bulk of engineering would be done outside the main living area by astro-engineers using an array of specialized equipment. On the sunward end of each cylinder would be a solar power station.

You would enjoy your leisure-time in ways which would be impossible on Earth. All transport within the 'habitats' would be non-polluting. You would ride in electric runabouts, plying between townships, schools and countryside; though most people would use bicycles for sightseeing.

In the largest colonies, artificial

mountains could be built near the end dome, with all the facilities for winter sports. Rivers would meander through the valleys and you could take a boat out on one of the lakes, or just sit by the bank with your fishing rod.

Long ago, endangered species of animals would have been transferred to a 'space station' for preservation, in a 21st-century version of Noah's Ark.

Now they roam freely in carefully simulated natural surroundings, far from the danger of pollution, urban sprawl or man's cruelty and greed. You can feed the African elephants, laugh at the pandas or thrill to the simmering ferocity of the Bengal tiger, all species which, by then, may be extinct on Earth.

For food purposes there would be no need to ship out large consignments of animals from Earth farms or stockyards.

Livestock is improved by artificial insemination, and all that is needed to replenish plant stocks are seeds.

Feeling too energetic merely to wander round the 'space zoo'? Sport and recreational activities would be given an exciting new impetus with the different grades of artificial gravity the colony could provide. Climbing hills and mountains, for example, would become easier the higher you went. At the top, you may experience only 0.1g (one-tenth of normal gravity). You could don wings and achieve mankind's great dream of flying like a bird . . . or make a slow-motion dive into a hilltop swimming pool.

In a low-gravity theater, ballet-dancers could fly like angels in dreamlike choreographical fantasies, and in a zero-gravity stadium you could cheer-on your favorite team playing three-dimensional baseball, basketball or football. The players would be able to swoop and dive in mid-air, helped by nitrogen gas jets strapped to their backs.

Keeping in Touch

'News from home' would be no problem. In terms of broadcasting, Mother Earth is just 1.3 seconds away, and there would be a constant exchange of TV programs. You would never feel 'cut off' from home, as every kind of information would be available on video screens, merely by dialing into a computer.

Information about relatives back on Earth, home-town news, reviews of the Arts, even the latest sports scores—all could be fed to your video machine far quicker than you could tune into your favorite TV channel now.

Traveling between one habitat and

Life in space might take some getting used to: one NASA design for a space colony has three 'continents' running the length of a gigantic cylinder, separated by windows to the sky. The inhabitants would look up and see not clouds but more land.

another to meet the 'neighbors' is just a simple matter of getting into a 'space taxi', casting off from one of the habitat's revolving arms—or docking points—and drifting to your destination. Your space taxi docks automatically under computer control.

You could go on 'vacation' the same way, maybe to specially created 'leisure habitats', giant cylinders designed to recreate all the exciting variety provided by earthly pleasure-resorts. In one controlled area, you could relax in a

Polynesian climate with atolls, beaches, gentle surf and palm-frond huts; or there could be a 'space Switzerland' of gentle, pine-clad slopes, quaint villages with onion-dome churches and even the occasional grazing cow.

You can make the 'day' as long as you like and turn up the amount of sunlight simply by programming the central computer. You can 'warm' the lakelike inland seas and provide flamingos instead of herons and gulls; make bougainvillaea bloom or citrus trees burgeon with oranges.

Almost anything you can dream of you can have . . . once you have taken that first, frontier-building step into outer space. But why space cities in the first place? What combination of circumstances is forcing scientists to look away from Earth and toward the Moon?

The whole science-fact concept of 'Cities in the Sky' really started in 1969, when Dr. Gerard K. O'Neill—a professor at Princeton University and the acknowledged 'father' of space colonies—was questioning his students on the value of further technological growth on Earth. To many of the students the future for Earth-bound mankind looked bleak. Science and technology were in disrepute. The world faced shortages of valuable natural resources and there seemed no way to stem the tide of pollution.

Moon Mining

O'Neill's solution staggered the imagination. He calmly asked if it were not possible—within the limits of present-day technology—to transfer sections of industry into space to exploit raw materials on the Moon and later the asteroids and other planets.

The more O'Neill investigated the subject, the more he realized that the 'City in the Sky' would not only be a perfect habitat, it could also immeasurably improve conditions for everyone back on Earth . . .

Space colonies could tap the Sun's raw energy in space—an inexhaustible, non-polluting energy source—to transform lunar ore into structural materials.

They could contribute to the world's food supply by beaming energy to Earth. Huge power-conversion satellites, built by the space colonists from lunar materials, would collect energy from the Sun and transmit it to Earth receiving-stations in the form of microwaves for conversion to electricity. Apart from ordinary domestic use, this would provide underdeveloped countries with unlimited sources of low-cost energy for making chemicals needed in high-yield agriculture.

By narrowing the need for the strip-mining of coal and our dependence on oil, they could improve the Earth's endangered environment. Waste heat

released into Earth's biosphere from major industrial processes would be lessened—so reducing the chances of bringing about disastrous climatic changes and cutting the amount of pollution in the environment generally.

The seemingly unstoppable build-up of nuclear materials would be halted, thus dampening the likelihood of nuclear accidents and nuclear terrorism.

Earth economy would be stimulated by developing non-military products of a new and exciting type in the zero-gravity, hard vacuum environment of space—using raw materials obtained from the Moon and eventually other bodies in the Solar System.

In short, our space colony could represent a new Utopia—the perfect life that mankind has dreamed of for centuries—and a blessing to those 'left behind'.

At the time, O'Neill's ideas seemed revolutionary. While most scientists were willing to concede the value of ordinary space stations for advancing science and technology, the thought of moving whole communities of people into a 'limbo' nearly 250 000 miles away from Earth seemed fanciful.

His early Model 1 space colony, sketched in 1974, was boldly conceived to accommodate 10 000 people. He suggested it should be established at one of the all-important Lagrange Points (L.5), where the gravitational fields of Earth and Moon are in equilibrium.

Later, O'Neill drew plans for much larger colonies, miles across and housing more than one million inhabitants. Encouraged by his enthusiasm, other scientists worked on 'wheel-shaped' designs, over a mile in diameter, which would simulate Earth's gravity by rotating at their hub once every minute. Facilities like stores, schools, light industry and agriculture would be contained on the 'rim'.

The question everyone asked was: How could one build such structures?

O'Neill explained that such projects would be out of the question if you had to launch every scrap of material from the deep gravitational 'well' of the Earth. One would have to exploit as much of the raw materials in space as possible.

But O'Neill's ideas really gained momentum as a result of the first Moon landings. At the time of the early Apollo projects, scientists did not think of the Moon as a vast, untapped source of raw materials. But the Moon landings in 1969/70—originally motivated by national pride and a sense of adventure—developed into scientific expeditions. Until then, nobody could plan in a rational way to run a program of space colonization until the Moon's mineral potential was established. Everything hinged on the lunar samples.

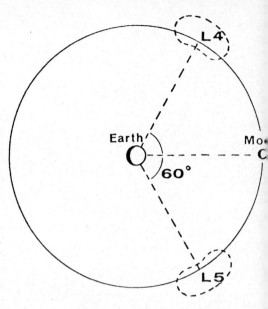

The ideal positions for space cities would be at L4 and L5, gravitationally null points in the Moon's orbit.

The result excited scientists all over the world—and delighted O'Neill. On analysis, a typical soil sample collected by Apollo 11 was found to contain 40 percent oxygen, 19.2 percent silicon, 14.3 percent iron, 8 percent calcium, 5.9 percent titanium, 5.6 percent aluminum and 4.5 percent magnesium.

According to O'Neill's figures, more than 95 percent of materials required for the 'Island One' city in the sky could be taken directly from the Moon, processed in space and used for construction purposes. Only hydrogen, carbon and nitrogen needed to be flown out from Earth.

There was another 'bonus'. The energy to bring materials from the Moon is 1/20th as much as from the Earth.

O'Neill is convinced the task can be done—even in terms of present-day technology. The cost, of course, would be staggering. Scientists estimate that it would need at least $100–150 billion to establish 'Island One' in space—with the pioneering 'colonists' leaving for their new home by the turn of the century.

They would be the new 'space frontiersmen', paving the way for the later and more ambitious colonies.

There, then, is the clearly-emerging shape of Utopia-to-come. But enormous problems have to be solved. First, the obvious one of *how* we can construct a new Colony in Space, even of the simplest kind. Later, there will be stranger obstacles to overcome. For in the wonderland environment which will one day develop—where you can simulate Alpine skiing one moment and bask on a Caribbean beach the next—would there still be some vital, human element missing?

CHAMBER OF HORRORS

What is the terrible secret of the 'hidden room' in Glamis Castle which, according to legend, is revealed to the eldest son on his 21st birthday? It is whispered that the chamber contains the remains of a monstrous creature born to the family. Others say it holds the bodies of prisoners forced by starvation into cannibalism. Whatever the secret, it could provide the clue to the curse which has hovered over the Strathmores for generations.

Hulton Picture Library

The accursed Glamis Castle, home of the Strathmore family for generations.

The heavy, oak door swung open easily under the workman's hand. In front of him extended a long, dark passage, apparently on a slight incline. The workman—lost in the labyrinthine corridors of ancient Glamis Castle, in Scotland—started downwards. He had only taken a few steps before he experienced a feeling of claustrophobic evil. What he saw next almost made him retch in terror.

He fled from the scene, stumbling blindly along the castle's passageways. In London, the news of the workman's mysterious 'discovery' was relayed to the owner of the castle, Lord Strathmore, the grandfather of Britain's present Queen Mother.

The Lord of Strathmore returned immediately to Glamis and, in strict secrecy, cross-examined the workman on what he had seen. A few months later, the workman emigrated from Britain with his family . . . at the expense of Lord Strathmore.

Nothing more was ever said. Only whispered. For the workman—or so it was rumored—had unwittingly stumbled on one of the world's most strange and sinister secrets; the eerie 'Locked Room of Glamis' which holds the clue to the curse which the Strathmores have borne for generations.

An earlier Earl of Strathmore once told a friend, "If you could guess the nature of the secret you would go down on your knees and thank God it were not yours." And the records of Britain's Society of Psychical Research confirm that, after the inquisitive workman had been paid to leave the country, "Lord Strathmore was quite a changed man, silent and moody, with an anxious, scared look on his face."

With its conical towers and ornamental battlements, Glamis Castle looks like something out of a Walt Disney fairytale. But this sprawling, red-brick fortress has a reputation as one of the most haunted houses in the British Isles, with a history of murder and tragedy that extends back for almost a thousand years. The shadow of its curse, all the more potent because of its secrecy, still falls over the present owners, the Strathmores.

Murder Most Foul

It was here, in 1034, that King Malcolm II was stabbed to death by conspirators. The murderers died a few hours later when they tried to gallop over a frozen loch and the ice gave way. Malcolm's blood soaked so deep into the floorboards that no amount of scrubbing would remove it and the floor finally had to be re-boarded several generations later.

Six years afterwards—according to William Shakespeare—Macbeth murdered King Duncan the First at Glamis Castle. The room is still known as Duncan's hall.

Yet the uncanny record of hauntings and curses really gathered momentum three centuries later. The mansion of the Lyon family at Fortevist contained an ancient cup that was regarded as the greatest of the family treasures. Legend declared that anyone who removed it from the mansion would be accursed, but in 1372 Sir John Lyon married the daughter of King Robert II and decided to brave the hoodoo. When they moved into Glamis—a wedding present from his father-in-law—he took the cup with him. It was a big mistake. Eleven years later he was killed in a duel.

The curse had now gained a foothold. In 1573, John Lyon, Lord Glamis, was accused of plotting to poison the king, James VI. His wife, son and an old priest were also accused, though the whole 'plot' had been concocted by a jealous relative, William Lyon. Lord Glamis plunged to his death while trying to escape from Edinburgh Castle and his wife was burned alive in front of a gloating crowd. The son's execution was luckily delayed until his 21st birthday, by which time the repentant William Lyon had confessed that his accusations had all been lies.

The ghost of a lady in gray, which has

been seen by many people—including, it is said, the present owners—is thought to be that of Joan Douglas, Lady Glamis.

Glamis Castle, indeed, has ghosts round almost every corner. Historians and psychic investigators have lost count of the apparitions recorded by witnesses. There is a white lady who walks along the avenue, a tall and cadaverous-looking specter known as Jack the Runner, and a Negro pageboy.

Guests have spoken of strange figures entering their bedrooms at night and shouts and banging noises from the older parts of the castle. At the turn of the 20th century, Mrs MacLagan, wife of the Archbishop of York, described how she and another guest had simultaneous dreams about a bearded man with a 'dead face'. Later, Lady Strathmore confirmed that a man answering to that description had died in irons in the castle in 1486.

Another guest came down to breakfast and mentioned casually that she had been awakened by the banging and hammering of carpenters at 4 a.m. There was an awkward silence, then Lord Strathmore told her there were no workmen in the castle. She had heard one of the family ghosts.

The Queen Mother spent her childhood in Glamis, and is believed to have seen the ghost of the Negro pageboy. During the redecoration of her apartment, the Queen Mother once occupied the Blue Room and had to change her quarters because she was constantly disturbed by rappings, thumps and footsteps.

The Monstrous Heir

The best-known legend of Glamis— that of the 'Monster' or 'Horror'— dates from only 1800. In that year, says the legend, Lady Strathmore gave birth to a monstrously deformed child. As the first-born, the child should have been heir to the estates, but this was out of the question. Instead, the atrocious creature was confined in a secret chamber and kept there for the remainder of its life.

The secret was known only to the Earl, the heir to the title and one close friend of the family—usually the estate 'factor', or agent. One factor, Mr Arthur Ralston, could never be persuaded to stay the night in the castle, and when a later Lady Strathmore asked him about the mystery he told her, "It is lucky that you do not know and can never know it, for if you did you would not be a happy woman."

Nearly all the 'monster' legends—and there are many versions—link up with the all-pervading Curse of Glamis, and the mysterious 'secret room' which so terrified the blundering workman.

Does the room contain the remains of

Fussy Victorian furnishing beneath the arched Gothic ceilings at Glamis.

Mansell

the grotesquely deformed heir to the title, who was said to have perversely outlived several generations? Or is there something even more frightful immured within the walls of Glamis?

Local inhabitants claim that in the old days of clan feuds a party of Ogilvies fleeing from their enemies the Lindsays came to Glamis pleading for shelter and protection. The Lord of that day led them into a chamber deep in the recesses of the castle and, locking them in, left them there to starve. Their skeletons— some in a hideous state of semi-embalment—lie there to this day, preserved, they say, in the act of cannibalism, some

even gnawing the flesh from their own arms.

Each heir of Glamis, it is claimed, is told the secret under oath not to divulge it and taken to the hidden room on his 21st birthday. No woman, not even the wife of the owner, may know the secret of the chamber and the Queen Mother, though sometimes asked by intimate friends, will never speak of it.

According to one account, a previous Earl managed to trace the chamber by following the uncanny shouts and bangs to their source—but what he saw when he forced open the door made him collapse in terror. The room was resealed and its location kept a secret. At the beginning of this century, during a house party, some guests decided to

Nearby Cortachy Castle also has its ghost—the phantom drummer who heralds the death of members of the Airlie family.

locate the chamber by a simple trick: they hung towels from every window in the castle and then crowded outside to see the result. High in the battlements, one window had no towel hanging from it . . . but no amount of searching in the rabbit warren of corridors could reveal the hidden door.

Another version of the 'curse' puts the blame on a 15th-century Earl who defied the devil. Playing cards late on Saturday night with a friend—the notorious Earl of Crawford—Lord Glamis ignored his servants' warning that it was almost the Sabbath. They swore they would not cease playing until the game was finished, 'though they might continue till the crack of doom'.

No sooner had they uttered the oath than the clock struck midnight and a stranger in a black cloak appeared in the room and intoned that he would hold them to their word. Every year on the anniversary of that night, the two accursed players meet in the hidden room to continue the game which will only end on the Day of Judgement.

Absurd though it may sound, in 1957 a servant at the castle, Florence Foster, claimed to have heard the demon gamblers at their unholy game, "rattling the

dice, stamping and swearing." Often, she said, she had "lain in bed and shaken with fright."

Although the Lyons of Glamis appear to hold something of a baleful record, they are only one of many families on whom there seems to be a persistent curse or jinx which defies explanation.

In nearby Forfarshire there is another castle with a long and malevolent history. The ghost of Cortachy Castle, the seat of the Earl of Airlie, announces the imminent death of any member of the Airlie family by performing on a drum.

Drummer of Doom

In 1845 Miss Margaret Dalrymple and her maid, Ann Day, were on a visit to Cortachy. During dinner she remarked on the strange music she had heard coming from below her window as she had dressed . . . the sound of a fife, followed by drumming.

It was *quite* the wrong thing to say. The other guests fell silent and Lady Airlie looked distressed. After dinner another guest explained that the sound of the diabolical drummer heralded the death of someone in the family and the last time it had been heard was just before the death of the Earl's first wife.

The next morning, the maidservant, Ann Day, was alone in Miss Dalrymple's room while everyone was at breakfast. She heard a coach drive into the court-yard and looked out of the window. To

her surprise, the courtyard was empty; but as she turned away she heard a drumming sound, apparently approaching from some distance. By the time the sound stopped, Ann Day was close to hysterics.

When Miss Dalrymple heard the drumming yet again, the following day, she decided she had had enough of Airlie and its ghosts. She packed her bags and left. Six months later Lady Airlie died in Brighton, leaving a note in which she said she was convinced that the drumming had signalled her own death.

Five years later the drummer announced the death of her husband, and in 1881 it was heard by Lady Dalkeith and Lady Skelmersdale just before they received the news of Lord Airlie's death in America. So far this century the drummer has refrained from performing his macabre melody.

Who was the drummer originally? One story claims he was a 'truce' messenger sent by the Lindsay family to the Ogilvies—the family name of the Earls of Airlie. The Earl of Airlie promptly tied him in a drum and threw him out of the window into the courtyard. As he fell, the drummer cursed the family into eternity. A more plausible story suggests that he was thrown to his death because he was Lady Airlie's lover; though a more refined version identified the murdered man as a ne'er-do-well brother of Lady Airlie, who was hurled

to his death when the Earl caught him trying to borrow money.

Strangely, there is still a drum in the room from which the man was said to have been thrown. The drumming certainly fits in with a current psychical-research theory that a 'ghost'—particularly an audible one—is nothing more than a kind of psychic 'tape recording' in which some powerful human emotion has somehow imprinted itself on its surroundings. Perhaps some retainer originally played the drum to cover the sounds of a violent quarrel. Yet it still fails to explain why the drum should only be heard before the death of a

When he evicted the monks from Battle Abbey, Sir Anthony Browne brought down their curse on his home, Cowdray House.

member of the Airlie family, and so far no 'scientific' explanation has succeeded in covering *all* the facts.

In the case of Glamis and Cortachy it seems fairly clear that the curse was associated with the house itself, supporting the 'tape recording' theory.

But how can one explain a curse that seems to follow the victims around, sometimes over the course of many centuries? That is what plagued the

Mar's Work—near Stirling, Scotland—was never finished, thus fulfilling the abbot's prophecy.

Montague family. One of their ancestors, Sir Anthony Browne, had expelled the monks from Battle Abbey—the famous abbey on the site of Britain's Battle of Hastings—in 1545. An angry monk cursed Sir Anthony, declaring that he 'would lose what he prized most' and that fire and water would one day bring about the extinction of his dynasty.

Sir Anthony was not impressed. To add insult to injury, he went on to build a magnificent home, Cowdray House, on lands that had been confiscated from the Church near Midhurst, in Sussex. When he lavishly entertained Queen Elizabeth there, it looked as though the old monk's curse had fallen flat. But shortly afterwards his only son died and Sir Anthony became a defeated and embittered man.

After his death, Cowdray House passed to his grandson and for the next 200 years the curse—with its enigmatic threats of fire and water—became a family legend. Then, in 1793, Viscount Montague tried shooting the rapids of Laufenburg, on the Rhine. He and his companion suddenly disappeared into the boiling spray and were never seen again. One week later, Cowdray House was burned to the ground.

Montague had no children, so the line came to an end. It had taken nearly three centuries for the curse to be fulfilled.

The dividing line between a curse and

a malign prophecy is delicate and indistinct. The same uneasy definition is involved in two of Scotland's most famous family curses, that on the Erskins of Mar and the Gordons of Gight.

The Erskine curse consists of a long Gaelic poem attributed to the Abbot of Cambuskenneth, whose lands had been seized by the 20th Earl of Mar. It begins by stating that the 'proud chief of Mar' would sit in the place of the king, but that his work would be accursed and never finished. It predicts a fire in which a member of the Erskine family would die, and that three Erskines would 'grow up never to see the light'. It foretells the day when their land would be given to strangers, horses would be stabled in their hall, and an ash tree would grow from the topmost tower.

Prophecy Fulfilled

The prophecies began to be fulfilled almost immediately. In 1571, Erskine became Regent of Scotland and guardian of James VI. He then began to build a magnificent palace near Stirling—now known as Mar's Work—but ill luck pursued the venture and it was never finished. The curse remained dormant until 1715, when the Earl of Mar raised an army to support the Old Pretender; after his defeat his lands were confiscated and given to strangers. The wife of a subsequent Erskine died in a fire, and three of her children grew up blind. After the fire, the family home was deserted, and some marauding soldiers

stabled horses in the hall. As late as 1815, an ash sapling began to grow at the top of the tower—a sign that the curse was nearly at an end. And, in fact, the Erskines were restored to their estates in 1822.

The curse of the Gordon family was pronounced by a 13th-century seer called Thomas the Rhymer, who declared that when the herons left the trees the Gordons would lose their lands and three men would die violently. But it was *500 years* before the herons ceased nesting in Gight, and Katherine Gordon married a handsome gambler called Captain John Byron, known as Mad Jack. His excesses soon brought the estate to ruin, and it was seized by creditors and sold. Shortly afterwards, Lord Haddo was thrown from a horse in the grounds of the castle and broke his neck; the same happened to a servant a few weeks later. The final death was of a workman who was jeering about the curse when the wall under which he was seated fell on him.

The son of 'Mad Jack' Byron was a crippled boy named George. When he was 23 he wrote an autobiographical poem in which he described himself as a man laboring under a curse. It was called *Childe Harold*, and it made George Gordon—Lord Byron—famous. But a mere 12 years later his gloomy forebodings about his own destiny were fulfilled when he went to Greece to join the freedom fighters and died of rheumatic fever. With his death the strange curse of the Gordons came to an end.

Mary Evans

IS THIS A PHOTO OF CHRIST?

The photographer was amazed when he developed the negative. Clearly imprinted on it was the face of Christ. For the first time, the venerated Shroud of Turin had revealed its secret . . . only to be greeted with angry accusations of 'fake'.

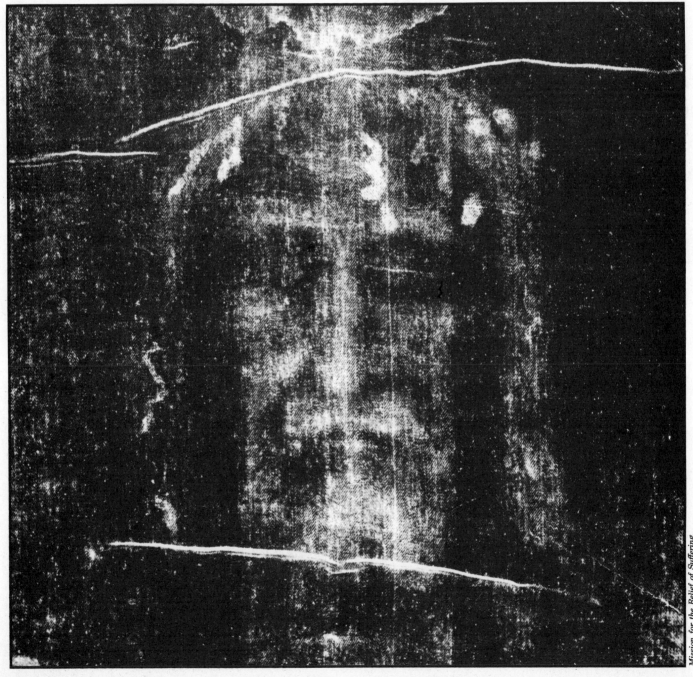

Mission for the Relief of Suffering

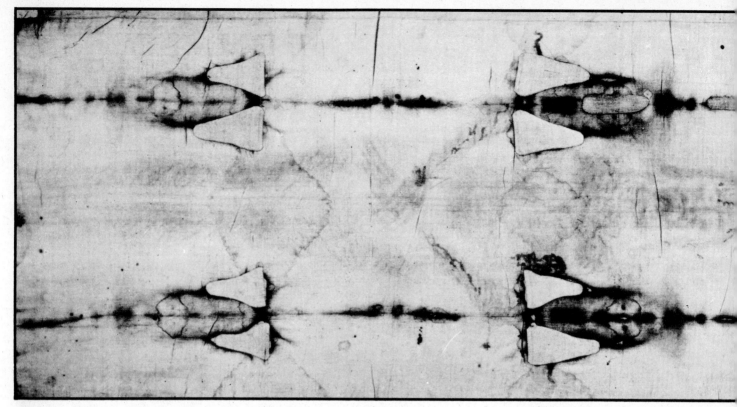

On a Friday night at the end of November 1973 millions of Italians turned on their television sets to watch what the Vatican called 'a televisual act of veneration'. They were allowed a rare look at the controversial Shroud of Turin—the stained linen garment said to have been wrapped around Christ's body after his Crucifixion.

The last time the Shroud—a yellowish relic measuring some $14\frac{1}{2}$ feet by $3\frac{1}{2}$ feet—had been seen in public was in 1933. Since then it had been under close guard in a closed silver casket in the Guarini Chapel of Turin Cathedral, where in 1971 it had been the subject of a secret scientific examination by a team of anonymous experts—including a chemist, a biologist, and a blood specialist from Britain.

The result of the tests had not officially been made known. But the Vatican authorities vigorously denied reports that the Shroud was a fake—and that it had been forged in the 14th century by a painter and fabric-weaver in France.

It was to end such 'unfounded and irreligious statements' that the Archbishop of Turin, Cardinal Michele Pellegrino, decided to lend the Shroud to a TV team for a 30-minute documentary. The Vatican newspaper *L'Osservatore Romano* advised its readers to watch the program, and to view 'the relic in all its eloquent simplicity.'

The Turin Shroud has a history going back more than 1900 years, and it reached Turin in 1578 after being moved from Palestine, to Turkey, to what is now south-east France. However, it wasn't until two centuries later that it really became an international religious talking-point. Until then its authenticity had been taken as a matter of faith, and no one thought to—or was allowed to—examine it in detail.

Then, in 1898, a photographer named Seconda Pia was permitted to take some pictures of the Shroud. Like most Italian Catholics, he knew the usually stated facts about the piece of cloth—that it was of a herring-bone weave of the kind much in vogue at the time of Christ's life ... that it bore some scorch marks from a fire in which it was almost destroyed at Chembery Castle, the property of the House of Savoy, an Italian royal family ... that it was marked with myrrh and aloes, the ointments used on Christ's wounded body.

Negative Image

However, as Pia developed his negatives, and held them up to the light, he gasped with amazement. Though many had examined the stains through the centuries, their significance had remained hidden until light and shade were reversed. Pia's negatives clearly showed a face imprinted on the Shroud—the face of a man of about 33, with a short divided beard, moustache, and shoulder-length hair.

The face, apparently, was that of Christ's as it was in his last agony. Two years after Pia's startling discovery—and after much behind-the-scenes discussion—the photographs were given to the French surgeon and forensic scientist, Dr Yves Delage, for *his* opinion of the Shroud's authenticity.

A freethinker, Delage—who was used to conducting autopsies on the bodies of murder and guillotine victims—accepted the fact that the reddish-brown stains on the cloth resembled the front and back views of a tall and well-built man.

To his mind, however, this didn't mean that the body had been Christ's. It was only when he put the Shroud under his microscope that he saw something which professionally intrigued him. As he expected, the marks proved to be bloodstains—some of which had come from a wound on the victim's right side ... just about where Jesus had been stabbed with a Roman spear while on the Cross.

Delage was particularly impressed by the noble expression on the face imprinted on the cloth and decided to share his work with another forensic expert, Dr Paul Vignion. For the next 18 months the two men minutely examined the photographs, which showed that the crucified man had been tortured and beaten about the face and body.

Then, in April 1902, Delage sent his conclusions to the journal of the French Academy of Sciences. He was soon invited to give his views in person, and a short while later stood somewhat apprehensively in front of an audience of his peers—all of whom were skeptical of anything which smacked of 'unscientific mysticism'.

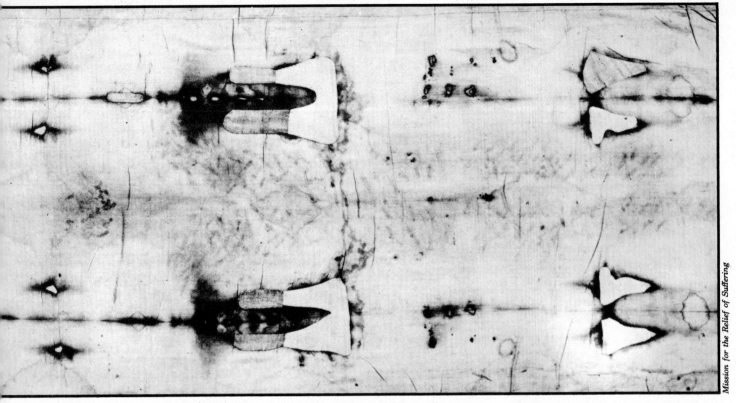

Mission for the Relief of Suffering

However, as Delage addressed them in an unemotional, matter-of-fact voice, they sat intently forward. There was total silence as he stated how the shoulders on the image bore wounds which corresponded with carrying a large and heavy object . . . how the knees were cut as if from bad falls . . . how the torso and thighs were covered with scourge marks, suggesting that a Roman *flagrum*—a double-thonged lash—had been used.

Behind the heel of each hand were nail wounds—which differed from most medieval paintings in which the nails were showed as going through Christ's palms. However, the victim's weight would have caused the flesh to tear so that the nails would, in reality, have been insufficient to keep the body up.

In addition to this, the thumbs on the Shroud figure were retracted into the palms of the hands—which is what would happen if nails were driven through the median nerve, which runs down through the middle of the wrist.

"On the one hand," Delage told his spellbound listeners, "we have the Shroud, impregnated with aloes —which brings us to the East outside Egypt—and a crucified man who has been scourged, pierced on the right side and crowned with thorns, as marks on the forehead indicate.

"On the other we have an account —pertaining to legend, history, and tradition—showing us Christ as having undergone the same treatment as we decipher on the body whose image is on the Shroud.

"For once, in such discussions, the two hands are not in opposition to each other. They appear to combine to give the conclusion that the crucified man and Christ are one and the same."

There was a quick buzz of comment at this. But Delage quelled it by pointing out that, scientifically, for such marks to be made on a shroud the body would have to be wrapped in it for at least 24 hours—and that it would have to be removed within three days before putrefaction set in.

The Seamless Shroud

This, he continued, tallied with the belief that Christ rose from the dead on the third day, so leaving the seamless Shroud behind him. If this was so—and if Delage's conclusions were correct—then the Turin Shroud was, in all probability, all that the Vatican claimed it to be.

"Christ," he stressed, "died on Friday and disappeared on Sunday. If the image is not of him, then it must be that of some contemporary of his—a criminal found guilty and crucified under the common law.

"Yet how is this to be reconciled with the admirably noble expression which you can plainly see on the figure? Christ died so that others should live, and, knowing this, he realized that his end was cruel but inevitable. It was the will of God so that others should benefit by it."

After repeating the five 'significant circumstances', which had so impressed

The Holy Shroud—marked with stains of fire and water and with the faint outline of a man's body, full length front and back. The custom of the Jews was to lay the corpse along the length of the shroud then fold it over at the head, so that the negative image of the face (opposite page) appears joined to the back of the head (this page).

him—the East outside of Egypt; the spear wound in the right side; the Crown of Thorns; the duration of the burial; the character and disposition of the face—he stated:

"Suppose that for each one there should be a chance in 100 that it would occur in the case of another person. There would then be only about one chance in 10 000 million that all these conditions should occur together in the case of a person who was *not* Christ."

This was a remarkable statement to come from as pragmatic a person as Dr Delage. But his words convinced nearly everyone present, and he sat down to a tumult of applause—applause which still echoes on today.

His only opponent in the room was Monsieur Berthelot, the permanent secretary of the Academy, who refused to put Delage's findings to the vote. However, the *Revue Scientifique* came out in his favor, and he later gained support in the editorial columns of the London *Times*.

By then, however, his enemies'—including such prominent Catholics as

Canon Ulysse Chevalier of France, and the British Jesuit, Father Thurston—had prepared a counter-attack on his views.

Quoting from an alleged confession of an impoverished painter to Bishop Henri of Poitiers, in the 14th century, they stated that the Shroud was a fake and that 'it was asking too much for intelligent, enlightened men to believe that it had survived several changes of ownership, to say nothing of a severe fire, since the time of Christ's Crucifixion.'

The Canon was particularly scathing of his fellow Frenchman, and declared that the 'former freethinker' had been fooled by "superstition and the egotistical conviction that his expertise could not be faulted." More than this, the Canon felt it 'wicked' to present such 'fantastical theories' as 'positive proof.'

"Over the centuries there have been too many such similar claims," he remarked. "Pieces of wood supposed to have come from the Cross have actually been peddled outside the great cathedrals of France, Italy and Spain. People must not be made fools of in this way. The subject is too awesome and profound to be allowed into the hands of mere forensic experts who, in a way, are putting Christ on trial again!"

14th-century Forger?

In response to this, Delage pointed out that the Shroud had been authenticated since the 14th century and that there was then no painter capable of executing such a perfect forgery.

"It is very difficult to admit of an image painted at that time as a positive," he said, "but when it is a *negative* image, which only assumes its values when the lights and shades are reversed, then we must say 'no'.

"Such an operation would be impossible except by the use of photography, an art unknown at that time. The forger, while painting such a negative, would have to know how to distribute light and shade so that after reversal they would give the figure of Christ in perfect and precise detail.

"Also, the bloodstains on the cloth are positive, whereas the rest of the representation is negative—a detail which surely even the most skilled of 14th-century artists could not have invented."

Delage's other main point, however, was not a scientific one, but one of emotion. "If it had not been Christ's image, but that of one of the Greek mythological heroes or Egyptian pharaohs," he stated, "then there would have been no objections.

"But, just because it is Christ, I fail to see why people should be scandalized because there exists a piece of material evidence of his existence."

From then on the controversy continued to attract defenders and attackers of the Shroud. For the next 60 or more years the Vatican maintained a discreet neutrality—although there was no doubt that the various Popes believed in the Shroud's authenticity.

It wasn't until the scientific examination in 1971—and the television 'performance' two years later—that the Roman Catholic Church openly stated its case. The Vatican's leading expert on the Holy Shroud at the time of the examination was the Right Reverend Giulio Ricci, who declared that the experts' findings had confirmed that the image on the linen was genuine.

"Each member of the commission is convinced that it is the Shroud of Christ," he said. "We are not making their findings known in a particular way, and I can only give a generalized summary of their conclusions.

"For instance, the position of the head and chin of the Shroud image show that

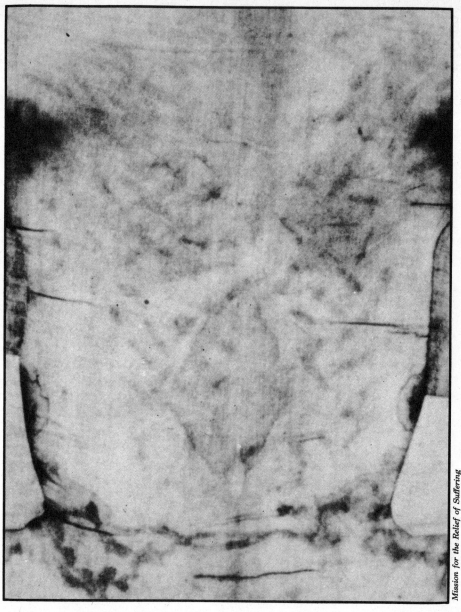

Mission for the Relief of Suffering

On the dead man's back—so the Shroud reveals—are the marks of the scourge. Whether or not the man was Christ, he had suffered the same fate.

rigor mortis took place at the exact position of a man on a cross. The conclusion was that he had been crucified.

"The linen of the Shroud was of a kind first produced at Antinoe, in the Middle East, at around 130 B.C. It is inconceivable that another man could have been wounded and wrapped in an identical way to that which the four Gospels describe as being the case for Jesus. This is our 'final proof'."

After seeing the television program, millions of viewers in Italy agreed with this verdict and declared that the controversy was at an end. The Holy Shroud of Turin was then reverently placed back in its casket to await its next public appearance—at some unspecified time in the future.

I COULD NOT BEAR ANOTHER LOSS...

Once more, a Kennedy was being carried to triumph in the polls. And again the nation asked, 'Will Teddy run for President?' Political power had already cost the lives of two of his brothers. The chance of history being cruelly repeated was even too much for their mother, who had seen the family curse bring nothing but sickness, disaster and death.

Popperfoto

It was a warm midsummer's evening in 1969 and a party had been planned. An outdoor cook-out for a dozen people at a small cottage on Chappaquiddick Island, a chunk of land east of the resort area of Martha's Vineyard in Cape Cod, Massachusetts. A party that started with cocktails and small-talk . . . and ended with death.

This time, the Kennedy involved in the tragedy was Teddy, youngest and only remaining son of Joseph P. Kennedy, patriarch of America's most ill-fated family. Once again the remorseless bad luck that had dogged the Kennedy Clan for so long struck cruelly and without warning.

The party was to say 'thank-you' to the 'boiler-room' girls, the third-echelon staff who had worked so devotedly for Bobby Kennedy's political campaign the previous summer. Bobby was now dead, assassinated like his older brother, President John F. Kennedy. Only Teddy was left to carry the burden of the Kennedys' political ambitions.

It was not a very jolly party. Everyone seemed tired from the day's various activities—Teddy had been sailing in a regatta with his nephew Joe Jr., and the ghost of Bobby Kennedy hung heavily over the proceedings.

The six men had not brought their wives because it was an office party. Teddy's wife, Joan, was two months pregnant anyway and resting up at their home in Hyannis Port.

The oldest of the 'boiler-room' girls, all respectable young women with impeccable reputations, was a small slim blonde called Mary Jo Kopechne who was 28. The girls had been hand-picked for their jobs by Bobby Kennedy who chose them for their 'discretion, brains, loyalty and humor under strain.'

For the party, they had brought steaks to barbecue and there was vodka, scotch, rum and beer to drink, but nobody, according to later reports, got drunk.

It was, perhaps, around 11.15 p.m. when Teddy Kennedy announced he was leaving and asked his chauffeur, John Crimmings, for the keys to the Oldsmobile. He said he was going to drop off Mary Jo Kopechne at her motel on the mainland of Edgartown. The only way back to the mainland was by ferry which ran until midnight and later by special request. But neither Teddy Kennedy nor Mary Jo Kopechne took the ferry to Edgartown that night. Instead, driving towards the beach, in the *opposite* direction to the ferry, the Oldsmobile overshot a narrow wooden bridge with no guard rails and plunged into the pond.

More than eight hours later, the dead body of Mary Jo was discovered trapped in the upside-down car at the bottom of Poucha Pond.

The exact truth about the events on

that humid night of July 18 has never been fully revealed. Certainly Senator Edward Kennedy's version was vague and inconclusive and frequently contrary to the evidence.

Eight days after the accident, Kennedy appeared on television to give his side of the story, but he did little to clear up the mysteries. He denied "widely circulated suspicions of immoral conduct," refuted rumors that he had been drunk, and described how "the car overturned in a deep pond and immediately filled with water. I remember thinking as the cold water was rushing in around my head that I was for certain drowning. Then water entered my lungs and I actually felt the sensation of drowning. But somehow I struggled to the surface alive . . ." He then described his repeated dives to try to rescue Mary Jo.

But the questions went unanswered. Why was Kennedy driving towards the beach, away from the ferry, in the first place? Why did he wait until the following morning before reporting the acci-

dent? And could Mary Jo have been saved if he had reported it sooner?

Why, after returning to the cottage to enlist the help of his friends, did he claim he jumped in the river to swim across to Edgartown?

Ladies' Man

Weighing against Kennedy was his reputation as a ladies' man, a fast driver and a heavy drinker since Bobby's death. On television he said that his actions during the hours following the accident "make no sense to me at all." And he claimed that among the scrambled thoughts running through his mind at the time was the nagging question of "whether some awful curse did actually hang over all the Kennedys . . .?"

It is a question he and the rest of the family have had cause to ask again and again over the years.

Less than six weeks after the Chappaquiddick tragedy—shortly before the inquest on Mary Jo Kopechne—Joan Kennedy had her third miscarriage.

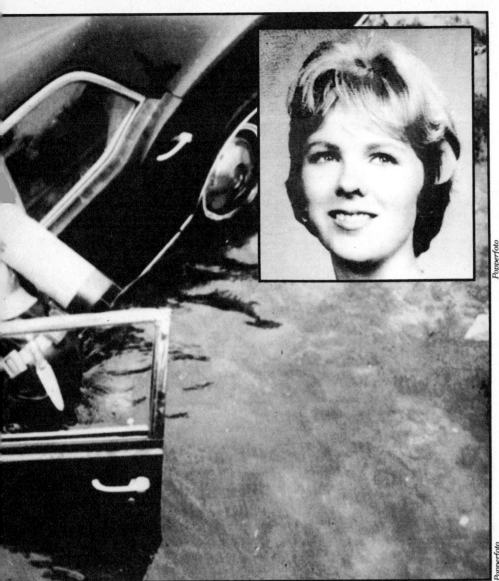

had never included the tragedies that had befallen them continually. Yet the two had gone hand in hand, as inseparable as daylight and darkness.

They had succeeded where others had failed and, in a way, much of their misfortune was the result of their success. They had become, probably, the most loved and most hated family in America.

Joseph Kennedy was buried in Brookline, Massachusetts beneath a simple granite slab engraved with the single word, 'Kennedy'. His grave was not far from the house where he and Rose started their family over 50 years before.

The family curse did not end—as many people hoped and prayed—with the death of 'Old Man Kennedy'. It was soon to be the turn of the younger members of the family . . .

Teddy threw himself into his Senate work, aiming for re-election in the 1970 primaries. More than ever he needed a convincing win, a sign that he had been forgiven for Chappaquiddick. In the event he won 62.6 percent of the vote, a sharp decline from his 74.4 percent of 1964, but a win nonetheless.

And now the question in everyone's minds was whether Teddy would follow in his brothers' footsteps and run for

The tragic incident at Chappaquiddick—which cost Mary Jo Kopechne her life—also proved to be the death blow for Joe Kennedy Sr., who gave in to his paralyzing illness and died 4 months later. At his funeral, Teddy was the only Kennedy son that remained to comfort his mother Rose.

And it was Chappaquiddick that proved the final, fatal blow to Teddy's father, Joseph Kennedy. His nurse, Rita Dallas, has said, "From that point on Mr Kennedy failed rapidly . . . we all knew it was only a matter of time."

For eight years Joseph Kennedy had been partially paralyzed as the result of a severe stroke and had been unable to walk or talk normally. Already he had outlived four of his nine children and each tragedy had been another unbearable blow. But it was Chappaquiddick which had truly broken his heart.

Writes Nurse Dallas in her book *The Kennedy Case*, "Toward late summer Mr Kennedy lost his appetite, and I knew he had given up. Over the years I watched him sometimes force himself to eat, but when he finally stopped, I felt my heart sink. He barely touched his food after Chappaquiddick."

On November 18, 1969, surrounded by his remaining family, Joseph P. Kennedy died at his home in Hyannis Port.

His dreams of greatness for his family

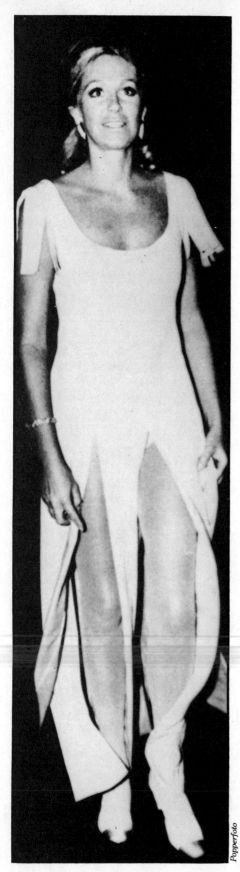

The gossip that surrounded Teddy Kennedy's role at Chappaquiddick threatened his marriage, as Joan seemed to retaliate with gestures of defiance to the Kennedy clan.

President. It was a possibility that terrified his family.

His mother, Rose Kennedy, wrote, "I did not want him to run. No one who really cared about him wanted him to . . . Even strangers would approach me and say, 'Don't let him, Mrs Kennedy.' The reason was altogether too obvious in view of what had happened in our family . . . I could not bear another such loss. And there were all those 16 children, Jack and Bobby's and his own, for whom he had a responsibility and who needed him."

And Teddy's wife, Joan, declared, "To have the one Kennedy man left risk having happen to him what happened to his brothers? Ted knows the Kennedys are not pushing him towards it."

In the meantime the rumors of the breakdown of Joan and Teddy's marriage gathered momentum. It was no secret that Teddy was seeing other women. By October 1972 one woman in particular was seen constantly in his company. She was jet-setter Amanda Burden, who was separated from her millionaire politician husband, Carter.

Illicit Romance

Speaking out for the first time Joan Kennedy said, "I'm bored to tears with gossip about Ted and his so-called illicit romances. But it does not hurt me. I have learned that 98 percent of it is either false or distorted."

By now Joan Kennedy was undergoing psychiatric treatment. "I realize now that I do not have to sweep things under the rug," she said. "I can hear unpleasant news and not let it upset my day."

The following year Joan was herself being escorted by a series of young male companions.

Divorce appeared to be out of the question for the couple because of their Catholicism and the welfare of their three children. Said Joan of the Kennedys, "For years I went along with everything they said because I didn't dare do otherwise, but now I speak up and say what I think and it seems to work out better for everyone. This family can be overwhelming."

The time had passed when Joan shocked Washington with her extreme outfits—micro-mini skirts, transparent blouses, cover-girl sweaters, which caused one amateur psychoanalyst to write, "Obviously she is projecting her inner conflicts." But even her new-found independence seemed not to bring her contentment. She started drinking heavily and spent time in hospital being treated for 'psychiatric problems'.

And in the way that the Kennedy curse had passed down through the decades, so it began to affect the new generation of young Kennedys.

Twenty-eight in all, including the two

babies adopted by Jean Kennedy and her husband Stephen Smith, they had grown up in the shadow of a legend.

The Kennedys have so often been described as America's equivalent to a royal family, and living up to royalty has always been a strain for the offspring. As in the case of Robert Kennedy Jr., 16-year-old 'hippie' son of Bobby Kennedy, who in 1970 was charged with possessing marijuana. Found guilty with him was his cousin Robert Sargent Shriver III, son of Eunice Kennedy. Both boys were placed on probation for a year.

Just a few days after the year was up, Robert Kennedy Jr. was in court again, this time for allegedly spitting ice-cream in a policeman's face. Kennedy appeared in court with long hair, wearing patched jeans, sandals and a denim shirt. He pleaded *nolo contendere*—neither guilty nor not guilty.

Police Lieutenant Frederick Ahern told Judge Henry Murphy that Kennedy's car was parked with the door open, blocking traffic on busy West Main Street, Hyannis, Massachusetts. Kennedy was standing on the pavement talking to a girl in the car. Ahern said he asked Kennedy to move the car but that he refused. Ahern asked him if he was drunk and alleged that Kennedy then spat ice-cream in his face.

The boy, who was sleeping rough in a secluded wooded area with other youths, was given a week to pay the $50 costs.

It was Robert's brother, Bobby Kennedy's eldest son, Joseph III, who was on board a Lufthansa Jumbo Jet when it was hijacked in February 1972 en route from India to Europe, packed with explosives, and forced to land in Aden.

Kidnapped?

For a time his family feared Joe was being kidnapped in retaliation for the imprisonment of Sirhan Sirhan, the Arab nationalist who killed his father. But it turned out that the jet with 127 people on board had been hijacked by a group of Arabs protesting against the Israeli occupation of Palestine.

After an uncomfortable couple of days, during which some of the male passengers were pistol-whipped, the passengers were released. "I've been scared before but never for so long," admitted Joe.

That summer he was in the news again when he failed to pay a turnpike toll in Boston and was fined $25. Then, the following March, he was injured in a three-car collision near the University of California at Berkeley. Police said one of the vehicles swerved into Kennedy's car.

A well-built six-footer, Joe's first taste of drama had occurred when his younger brother David was in danger of drowning in the strong currents off Malibu Beach, California. Joe dived into the

U.P.I.

Popperfoto

Popperfoto

heavy seas and rescued David—just hours before their father was assassinated.

That same year Joe was attacked by a bull while trying his hand at being a matador in Spain. He was treated for a head wound. And a few months later he was badly injured playing football at his private school in Massachusetts.

Early in 1973 Joe dropped out of college, explaining that he was not making any friends and "could get a better education out of school."

Then, in August, he was driving a Jeep with six passengers—five girls and his brother David—in the historic whaling port of Nantucket Island, Massachusetts, when the vehicle went out of control and overturned. David's back

was injured and two of the girls were seriously hurt. One of them, Mary Schlaff,. 22, had a broken pelvis and femur. The other, Pamela Kelley, 19, was crippled for life. The daughter of a local barman, Pamela suffered a fractured pelvis and was paralyzed below the waist. Two years later the Kennedy family gave her settlement of $100,000.

There were witnesses to testify that young Joe had been driving badly. One of them, Mr Merrill Lindsay, claimed that the Jeep came towards him on the wrong side of the road and that he had to swerve out of the way, skidding 86 ft. Another, Mrs Sandra Peterson, who was driving a sightseeing bus, said she saw the Jeep going very fast with "people hanging all over the top of it."

The Kennedy curse did not stop at the first generation: trouble—of one sort or another—has followed the 28 grandchildren. Bobby Jr. (top left) was charged with drug abuse and spitting at a cop in quick succession; Joe Jr. (top right) was hijacked and then turned over a Jeep, paralyzing one of the girl passengers.

The judge fined Joe Kennedy $100 for negligent driving and told him, "I am in the situation in which I am sitting in judgment on the son of Robert Kennedy, who I knew in Washington and admired very much. You had a great father and you have a great mother. Use your illustrious name as an asset and do a lot of good that I know you are capable of doing rather than coming to court like this."

It would appear that the judge's lecture made an impression on the rebellious Joe. He began to cash in on his heritage, working his own way up the political ladder. In 1976, aged 23, he ran his Uncle Teddy's election campaign from the home state of Massachusetts to the Senate, the youngest man ever to run a major political show in the U.S.

The cruellest blow to the young Kennedys befell Teddy Jr., when he was only 12. The middle child of Teddy and Joan's three children, tragedy struck young Teddy in November 1973, when it was learned that he had bone cancer and would have to have his leg amputated.

"Probably the hardest thing I have ever had to do was tell Teddy about the amputation," said his father. "He cried and I cried. Teddy had a very human reaction: fear."

The Kennedy Guts

Like all the Kennedys, young Teddy had always been a very active, athletic child. He loved to ski, swim, play football, sail. Now he might never be able to do any of them again.

But Teddy has something else as well: a legacy of courage and determination. The Kennedy guts. It was not long after the operation that he was out on the ski slopes with his father, learning to manipulate his artificial leg.

It was not just Teddy who was affected by his tragic illness. His mother, Joan, took it particularly hard. She was also fretting over her other son, Patrick, who had a severe and dangerous form of asthma that required taking steroids.

Joan suffered badly. She was admitted to a string of private clinics specializing in the treatment of alcoholics and the emotionally disturbed. Her marriage continued to be a subject for malicious gossip until it was necessary to publicly deny rumors of an impending divorce.

In July 1974, Teddy and Joan's eldest child, Kara, had her leg and foot crushed and badly bruised when her horse-drawn holiday caravan crashed into a wall in the southern Irish village of Croon. Although no bones were broken, an hour-long operation was necessary before Kara could leave hospital.

Through all the anguish, father Teddy was pushing ahead through his own political turmoil, haunted always by the shadow of Chappaquiddick and his family's history of tragedy.

After his leg amputation, Teddy Jr. is reputed to have begged his father not to run for President. It is a sentiment still echoed by the whole of the Kennedy Clan. For it seems that there is no end to their ill-luck. Always there is that strange hoodoo waiting to turn their victories to grief, bringing pain, misery,

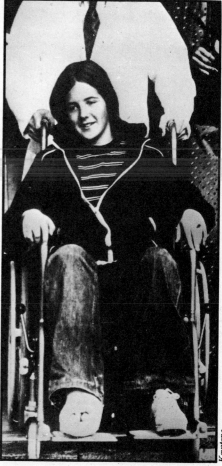

When Joe Jr. tried his hand at bull fighting, he ended up with a head injury. His cousin Teddy had to have his leg amputated in 1973, and in 1974 Teddy's sister Kara crushed her leg in a holiday accident.

and, all too often, death.

They have had their hours of glory, these incredible Kennedys, and they have paid dearly for every one of them.

In her autobiography, the indomitable Rose Kennedy says of her 28 grandchildren whose responsibility it now is to carry on the dynasty, "I hope they will have strength to bear the inevitable difficulties and disappointments and griefs of life . . . it isn't tears but determination that makes pain bearable."

A determination that gives the Kennedys a kind of grandeur.

When a monster says 'I love you . . .'

Creatures from outer space have feelings, just like anyone else. So it wasn't a surprise when artists started showing them falling for our women. Only the aliens didn't know when to stop.

1938: aliens start to get ideas . . .
1939: . . . and the trend catches on.
1940: togetherness on a spaceship.

'Take me to your leader' was what alien visitors were *supposed* to say when they set foot/claw/talon/hoof or suction-pad on our planet. But judging by the robust appetites of the creatures from outer space as seen by science fiction illustrators of the 1940s, 'Take me to your lady' would have been more appropriate.

For it was around that time that the Little Green Men discovered sex.

For decades, science fiction artists had depicted alien creatures engaging in every form of activity except 'following what comes naturally'. They had devastated Earth's cities, annihilated astronauts from our planet, terrorized whole civilizations, reduced the human race to vegetables and provided illustrators with an endless arsenal of sci-fi gadgetry.

But *never* a kiss from those bright green, iridescent lips.

It all changed when 'space artists' concentrated on showing human beings making friends with creatures on other planets. It was inevitable that, taking interplanetary good relations one step further, they should soon develop a taste for our woman.

As early as 1938, in the first issue of *Marvel*, a bat-like creature was shown drooling over an Earth-cutie, while her muscular hero leaped to the rescue.

A year later, in the December 1939

issue of *Science Fiction*, the police were doing the honorable thing by giving chase to a creature 'from the Planet of the Knob Heads' who had made off with a scantily-dressed charmer and was pounding along the freeway as fast as his pistons would carry him.

"Guns are useless!" cries one of the characters in the story, a fact confirmed by the bullets whanging harmlessly off old Knob Head's cranium in the illustration. Behind the creature, a skyscraper city blazes merrily. That mere destruction was not the object of the alien invasion is proved by a tiny Knob Head in the background, hot-footing back to base with yet another captive female.

Once illustrators had caught on to this novel boy-meets-ghoul twist, there was no stopping them.

A classic 'Look behind you!' bit of suspense was conjured up in Alex Schomburg's 1940s cover for *Future*. A blonde is attending to her toilet in (of all unlikely places) a spacecraft . . . while, unknown to her, a thoroughly scaly and repellent Little Green Man is climbing through the window with a look on his face which clearly doesn't say, 'Haven't you finished in the bathroom yet?'

To be fair to the aliens, their lustfulness is only exceeded by the sheer gormlessness of the women they get into their clutches. Virgil Finlay's luckless heroine on the April 1942 cover of *Famous Fantastic Mysteries* looks as though she is worried at mussing up her hair; not surprising, considering she is being snatched into the stratosphere by a leering monster.

That outer space is no place for a woman is a message which also rings loud and clear in A. Leydenfrost's 1953 *Tops in Science Fiction* illustration, where another reptilian alien (a reptalien, maybe?) has plucked a female from her spacecraft and is gazing at her with an expression which seems to say, 'Yes, but are they safe to eat?'

Interplanetary male chauvinism reached rock bottom with the Winter 1951-2 issue of *Science-Fantasy*, whose cover showed a damsel being carried off to Saturn by what looks like an ani-mated Roman statue, his finger pointing imperiously to their new home.

Yet oddly, the picture was the work of a talented woman, Ms R. M. Bull, to whom Women's Lib presumably meant as little as an ice-lollie to a polar bear.

Follow that! was what many artists must have felt, for the 'damsel in cosmic distress' cliché started to fade away.

It was time to sharpen those pencils afresh and return to the satisfying task of dreaming up weirder and more wonderful 'beasties'.

1942: (left) reptilian rapist.
1953: in alien clutches.
1951: they make a lovely couple.

GIVE UP THIS WOMAN OR LEAVE THE THRONE

At last the silence had been broken. Now the world knew about the romance between King Edward VIII and the twice-married Mrs Simpson. Establishment pressure mounted to force Edward to decide between the Crown and the American woman he loved. Could the King appeal to a sympathetic nation? It was his last and only chance . . .

Popperfoto

Popperfoto

John Frost

The Bishop of Bradford said yesterday that the benefit to be derived by the people from the King's Coronation would depend in the first instance on "the faith, prayer, and self-dedication of the King himself." Referring to the moral and spiritual side of that self-dedication, the Bishop said the King would abundantly need the Divine grace if he were to do his duty faithfully, and he added: "We hope that he is aware of his need. Some of us wish that he gave more positive signs of such awareness."

Dr. Blunt must have had good reason for so pointed a remark. Most people by this time are aware that a great deal of rumour regarding the King has been published of late in the more sensational American newspapers. It is proper to treat with contempt mere gossip such as is frequently associated with the names of European royal persons. The Bishop of Bradford would certainly not have condescended to recognise it....

In November 1936, King Edward VIII paid a visit to the officers and men of the British Royal Navy's Home Fleet in the port of Southampton. He was received with rapturous cheers and delighted the thousands of men packed into the underdeck of the aircraft carrier *Courageous* when he led a sing-song to the accompaniment of an able seaman's harmonica. It was yet another example of the King's universal popularity.

A few days later he returned to Fort Belvedere, still aglow with the memory of his reception in the Fleet, to find his butler in a state of fussy concern. Major Alexander Hardinge, the King's Private Secretary, had left a letter, the servant explained, and had especially asked that His Majesty should read it immediately.

Edward found it, lying on the top of the red boxes in which State documents were daily delivered to the Monarch, and was puzzled by the words 'Urgent and Confidential' on the envelope. He normally saw his aide almost every day and no matters of urgency had recently been mentioned.

When he had extracted the letter and begun to read it through, Edward

realized that it was one of the most momentous he had received in his life.

"As Your Majesty's Private Secretary, I feel it is my duty to bring to your notice the following facts which have come to my knowledge and which I *know* to be accurate," Hardinge wrote and, in numbered paragraphs, went on to outline those facts:

"(I) The silence of the British Press on the subject of Your Majesty's friendship with Mrs Wallis Simpson is *not* going to be maintained. It is probably only a matter of days before the outburst begins. Judging by the letters from British subjects living in foreign countries where the Press has been outspoken, the effect will be calamitous."

In paragraph two, Hardinge informed the King that Prime Minister Stanley Baldwin and his senior Government colleagues were meeting that very day, November 13, to discuss 'the serious situation which is developing' and which

might lead to their resignation. But the real shock to Edward came in Hardinge's concluding words:

"If Your Majesty will permit me to say so, there is only one step which holds out any prospect of avoiding this dangerous situation and that is for Mrs Simpson to go abroad *without further delay*, and I would *beg* Your Majesty to give this proposal your earnest consideration before the position has become irretrievable. Owing to the changing attitude of the Press, the matter has become one of great urgency."

What was so terrible about the bachelor King's friendship with the American-born Mrs Wallis Simpson and why had it generated such an alarming letter? The truth was simple. Mrs Simpson had divorced *two* previous husbands. By the unbending moral code of the time she was a 'tainted woman', though she had been the innocent party in each case. The attitude of the 'Establishment' was as clear as it was unforgiving: such a woman was totally unfit to be Queen of England.

Edward was stunned. Here was his Private Secretary—a servant, however exalted his rank in the hierarchy of the Royal Household—presenting the King with what amounted to an ultimatum: exile the woman you love if you wish to save your throne.

The King's mind leapt to one over-whelming conclusion. Baldwin *must* be the man behind the warning—Baldwin, determined that while he was Prime Minister Edward would never make Wallis his Queen, was using Hardinge as a lever. Perhaps it was a cunning test of the depth of his attachment to Wallis? But, if Baldwin was holding up the threat of the Government's resignation to induce him to part from Wallis Simpson, the Prime Minister had misjudged his man.

He spent a sleepless night, and the next day, brooding over the letter and then showed it to Wallis, saying, as she read it, "To use a good American expression, they are about to give me the works. They want me to give you up."

Ultimatum

She was as shocked by the ultimatum as he. And, perhaps for the first time, she saw the maelstrom into which their love was sweeping them as Edward took her hands in his and vowed that if the Government was as opposed to their marrying as Hardinge had suggested, then "I am prepared to go." Wallis begged him not to be impetuous. Maybe there was some other way to resolve this crisis.

At 6.30 on the evening of Monday, November 16, Stanley Baldwin ans-wered the King's summons to attend at Buckingham Palace. Dispensing with the usual formalities, Edward at once declared, "I understand that you and several members of the Cabinet have some fear of a constitutional crisis devel-oping over my friendship with Mrs Simpson."

That was so, the Prime Minister agreed, and added that, although some might think him 'a remnant of the old Victorians', even his worst enemy would acknowledge that he understood the people's reaction to events. And they would certainly find that a proposal by the King to marry Mrs Simpson was 'unacceptable'.

Giving full rein to the persistent ner-vous habit of brushing his right hand past his ear and snapping his fingers as he did so, Baldwin subjected the King to a baleful homily. His Majesty would appreciate that the position of the King's wife was different from that of the wife of any other citizen in the realm.

"It is part of the price a King has to

Popperfoto

pay," Baldwin intoned. "His wife becomes Queen, the Queen becomes Queen of the country and, therefore, in the choice of a Queen, the voice of the people must be heard."

The King listened, stonily, to this panegyric and, as Baldwin paused, said unhesitatingly, "I am going to marry Mrs Simpson and I am prepared to go."

There was a brief silence, broken only by the snap-crack of Baldwin's fingers, and then the Prime Minister solemnly replied, "Sir, this is most grievous news. It is impossible for me to make any comment on that today." The two men parted coldly, each aware that he had reached a historic political cross-road.

Some two hours later, Edward dined with his mother, Queen Mary. It was a deeply melancholy occasion. The widow-ed Queen, instinctively sensing an omin-ous tension in her son, struggled to keep the inconsequential table-talk alive. She congratulated Edward on his decision to have the outside of the Palace repainted; he responded by complimenting her on the progress of her favorite charity, the London Needlework Guild.

After the meal, when the servants had

(Left) Edward and Wallis at Balmoral before the abdication. (Below) the man who started the storm of publicity, Dr Blunt. (Above) Edward—still king—and his disapproving mother, Queen Mary.

been dismissed, the King broke the news of his meeting with Baldwin. Queen Mary listened in silent distress, no emo-tion visible on her austere features. Then, wistfully, she spoke of the sacred-ness of Monarchy and the duty of Kings. But the question, Edward insisted, was not whether Wallis was acceptable "but whether I am worthy of her."

As a last resort, the King appealed to his mother to meet Wallis Simpson. In his own, curiously unworldly way, he believed that, if only Queen Mary and Wallis could be friends, somehow every-thing would come right. But the Queen was adamant. He was utterly wrong to contemplate such a marriage and on no account would she meet Mrs Simpson.

The following day the King announced his marriage plans, and his intention to abdicate if that were un-avoidable, to his three brothers, the

Popperfoto

King Edward at Fort Belvedere, his favorite home in England. After the abdication he could never revisit it.

Dukes of York, Gloucester and Kent. For the eldest of the three, the shy Duke of York, the threat was especially agonizing. It meant that he might have to ascend a throne which he neither coveted nor felt himself prepared for.

Others now began to spin what they hoped would be useful threads. Esmond Harmsworth, son of Lord Rothermere, proprietor of the London *Daily Mail*, invited Wallis Simpson to lunch at Claridge's Hotel, in Mayfair. With Lord Beaverbrook, owner of the *Daily Express*, Harmsworth had helped to arrange the 'gentleman's agreement' on Press silence and he was, therefore, someone to whom Wallis would readily listen.

He had an unusual, but possible, 'solution' to advance to Wallis. Would she, he wondered, be prepared to enter into a morganatic marriage with the King? He explained that he meant a marriage between a Monarch and a woman of 'lesser birth' in which the wife would not

become Queen and whose children would have no right of accession to the Throne. Although he did not put it so bluntly, he was suggesting a marriage in which the parties might well become known as Edward VIII and Mrs Windsor.

Wallis Simpson was non-committal. It was not a subject on which she ought to comment, she said, but when she told Edward his spirits rose and he felt sufficiently enthusiastic to ask Harmsworth to try the idea out on Stanley Baldwin.

It was, however, nothing more than a pipe-dream. Baldwin dismissed the notion as preposterous. Quite apart from the fact that such a marriage would require a special Act of Parliament, which Parliament would not contemplate, the British people would never stand for it, he insisted.

Yet the unfortunate Prime Minister was unable to dispose of the idea so easily. Once more the King summoned him to the Palace and this time demanded to know if Mr Baldwin was really so certain that Parliament would refuse to consent to a morganatic marriage Act.

Wearily, Baldwin affirmed that he was quite certain, but, like Hamlet seeking

to trap the King, he smoothly slipped in a trick question, "Sir, would you like me to examine the question formally?" Edward eagerly agreed that he would.

In that case, Mr Baldwin was obliged to remind His Majesty that 'formally' meant there must be consultation not only with the British Cabinet but with the Cabinets of all the Dominions within the British Empire. Did the King really wish that, too? The King did wish it.

If there were any one point of no return in the whole drama that was it. The hook had been baited and the King had swallowed it. Now he was telling his Prime Minister that he sought to go over the heads of his own Imperial Government in the hope of finding allies elsewhere. It was a perilous move.

Now the time was ripe for Baldwin to play his ace card. He saw Clement Attlee, leader of the Socialists, and Sir Archibald Sinclair, of the Liberals—his official opponents in the House of Commons—and asked them, "If my Government is forced to resign over this matter would you support us or not?"

Volatile Issue

Attlee and Sinclair were unanimous. Neither of them, they promised, would vote against Baldwin or undertake to form an alternative government. It was not in their interests to come to power over the highly volatile issue of who might be 'for' or 'against' the Monarch —that would certainly divide the nation.

This was Baldwin's triumph. If the King had hopes of a possible eleventh-hour political 'solution', under a more amenable government, they were now doomed. And the Prime Minister had spice to add to his victory. The Dominions had told him they would not countenance a morganatic marriage.

At the beginning of September the veil of newspaper secrecy was at last torn aside. An obscure cleric, Dr A. W. F. Blunt, Bishop of Bradford, in the county of Yorkshire, delivered a generally unremarkable address to his Diocesan Conference in which he spoke of the forthcoming Coronation and of the need of the King, as of every man, to do his duty. But he added a sting to the tail, "We hope that he is aware of this need. Some of us wish that he gave more positive signs of such awareness."

Curiously, the big London newspapers let the comment pass, but, next day, an editorial writer in the Bishop's local *Yorkshire Post* linked it with current rumor 'in the more sensational American newspapers'. Of course, the tongue-in-cheek writer said, such gossip always surrounded thrones. Yet there had also been statements in reputable American journals, and some Dominion newspapers, which could not be treated with indifference. They were 'too circumstantial and plainly have a foundation in fact'.

This was good enough for Fleet Street's frustrated editors. Now that their Yorkshire colleagues had blown the whistle on the Edward-Simpson affair they could, officially, let the British people into the secret. Some were worried, but they need not have been. Readers were generally more astonished than angry and the most 'militant' reaction was confined to a few groups parading in London with placards reading, "God Save The King—From Baldwin."

Appeal to the People

Edward's first thought was to protect Wallis from the 'hounds of the Press'. He hastily arranged for her to be given sanctuary with friends in Cannes, in the South of France, and sent her there with his Lord-in-Waiting and his own, personal Scotland Yard detective. Wallis left him with hope of one last desperate move: why not make a broadcast to the people of Britain and the Empire, something on the lines of the 'fireside chats' that President Franklin D. Roosevelt had made so famous? Edward leapt at the idea and, in the absence of his beloved, worked excitely on his script.

Yet again, the exasperated Prime Minister was called to the Palace, this time to be confronted by an exhausted-looking King, parchment-pale, who pushed the draft of his radio speech into Baldwin's hands. Stanley Baldwin pretended to read the pages, with finger-snapping irritation. But, no, he declared, this would not do at all. The Cabinet would not accept a direct, personal appeal to the people—'it would be quite unconstitutional'.

The King's anger boiled over. "You want me to go, don't you?" he shouted at his astonished Prime Minister. "Well, before I go I think it is right for her sake and mine that I should speak!"

Baldwin did his best to assume an air of infinite patience. "What I want, Sir," he said, "is what you told me you wanted: to go with dignity, not dividing the country, and making things as smooth as possible for your successor. To broadcast would be to go over the heads of your Ministers.

"You would be telling millions throughout the world—among them a vast number of women—that you are determined to marry one who has a husband living. They will want to know about her and the Press will ring with gossip, the very thing that you want to avoid. You may, by speaking, divide opinion; but you will certainly harden it. The Churches are straining at the leash; only three newspapers would be on your side . . ."

The end was in sight; only the gloom of an epilogue remained. On the chilly

Popperfoto

John Frost

evening of December 3, Edward VIII left Buckingham Palace for the last time and took refuge in his beloved Fort Belvedere. Two days later his close friend and confidante, Sir Walter Monckton, informed Baldwin of the King's formal decision to abdicate.

In France, Wallis Simpson wrestled with the terrible weight of responsibility that had fallen upon her and, on Monday, December 7, she issued a statement to the world's Press, "Mrs Simpson, throughout the last few weeks, has invariably wished to avoid any action or proposal which would hurt or damage His Majesty or the throne. Today her attitude is unchanged and she is willing, if such action would solve the problem, to withdraw from a situation that has been rendered both unhappy and untenable."

Before the statement went out, Wallis called Fort Belvedere and told the King about it. There was a long silence—and then a voice, hoarse with fatigue, said, "Go ahead, if you wish—but it won't make any difference."

Baldwin made a final appeal to the

By a statement to Parliament, then by radio, the King gave his decision.

King—more for the polishing of the Government's image in posterity than in hope of success—and the King regretted that his decision was unalterable. Queen Mary, opened her heart with the cry, "To give up all *this* for *that*!"

On the morning of December 10, Edward VIII signed the Abdication document at Fort Belvedere and his three brothers added their signatures as witnesses. At ten o'clock he was King. At five minutes after ten he was a liegeman of His Majesty, King George VI, of Great Britain, Ireland and the British Dominions, and Emperor of India.

Now that he was no longer King, and history's page had safely turned, Edward was allowed to speak to his former subjects. From a temporary radio studio in the Augusta Tower of Windsor Castle he told the nation, in a strained voice, "You must believe me when I tell you that I have found it impossible to carry the heavy burden of responsibility and to discharge my duties as King as I would wish to do without the help and support of the woman I love."

The decision to go was his alone— "the other person most closely concerned has tried, up to the last, to persuade me to take a different course. I have made this, the most serious decision of my life, upon a single thought of what would in the end be best for all."

He commended his brother, the new King, to Britain and the Empire, and added a moving sentence that had been suggested by his friend Winston Churchill, "He has one matchless blessing, enjoyed by so many of you and not bestowed on me—a happy home with his wife and children . . . God bless you all. God save the King!"

Just a few hours after that broadcast, at two in the morning of December 11, the Royal Navy destroyer HMS *Fury*, slipped her cables in Portsmouth Harbor and carried Edward across the darkened English Channel to the French port of Boulogne and into exile.

Edward and Wallis were married on June 3, 1937, at the Chateau de Candé, near Tours, in France. She wore a 'Wallis blue' gown made in Paris and he a cut-away coat and striped pants. In accordance with French law, theirs was a civil ceremony but afterwards they were blessed by a Church of England clergyman. Both bride and groom were tense but Wallis managed one of her charming smiles for the camera.

One final, spiteful gesture by Authority in England had cast a shadow over the marriage. George VI had created Edward Duke of Windsor but had been obliged to insist that his wife would not be allowed to enjoy the title of 'Her Royal Highness'. She would be simply 'Duchess of Windsor' and women were not obliged to offer her the salutation of a curtsy. It was the final slamming of the door against a departed black-sheep.

After Edward had gone, the British Empire neither fell nor tottered, no one rioted in the streets and, a few months later, Baldwin was elevated to the peerage as the Earl of Bewdley, George VI went on to become one of the most popular monarchs in history and, even in exile, Edward and Wallis grew in the affection of the British people.

Their love and companionship endured, inviolate, for 35 more years until the Duke's death on May 28, 1972. Then Edward finally came back home and was buried at Windsor. And the British people were genuinely moved by the announcement that, when the time came, the Duchess would be laid to rest beside her husband. For old wounds had long healed, harsh words long been buried in dusty files, in the saga of the King who loved a woman who might have been Queen.

June 3, 1937: the wedding that had rocked the throne of England.